THE STONES OF VENICE.

THE STONES OF VENICE

INTRODUCTORY CHAPTERS AND LOCAL INDICES

(PRINTED SEPARATELY)

FOR THE USE OF TRAVELLERS

WHILE STAYING IN

VENICE AND VERONA

BY

JOHN RUSKIN, LL.D.

HONORARY STUDENT OF CHRIST CHURCH AND HONORARY FELLOW OF
CORPUS CHRISTI COLLEGE, OXFORD

VOLUME I

SEVENTH EDITION

GEORGE ALLEN, SUNNYSIDE, ORPINGTON

AND

156, CHARING CROSS ROAD, LONDON

1896

PREFACE.

This volume is the first of a series designed by
the Author with the purpose of placing in the
hands of the public, in more serviceable form,
those portions of his earlier works which he
thinks deserving of a permanent place in the
system of his general teaching. They were at
first intended to be accompanied by photographic
reductions of the principal plates in the larger
volumes ; but this design has been modified by
the Author's increasing desire to gather his past
and present writings into a consistent body,
illustrated by one series of plates, purchaseable
in separate parts, and numbered consecutively.
The note at page 147 in this volume, (lying
by during my illness,) referred to the smaller
photographs at that time in preparation : but
the extension of the plan will render all direc-

tions to the binder unnecessary, except such as the possessor of the book may himself issue. Of other prefatory matter, once intended,—apologetic mostly,—the reader shall be spared the cumber : and a clear prospectus issued by the publisher of the new series of plates, as soon as they are in a state of forwardness.

The second volume of this edition will contain the most useful matter out of the third volume of the old one, closed by its topical index, abridged and corrected.

BRANTWOOD,
    3rd May, 1879.

CONTENTS.

THE STONES OF VENICE.

CHAPTER I.

[FIRST, OF THE OLD EDITION.]

THE QUARRY.

§ 1. SINCE first the dominion of men was asserted over the ocean, three thrones, of mark beyond all others, have been set upon its sands: the thrones of Tyre, Venice, and England. Of the First of these great powers only the memory remains; of the Second, the ruin; the Third, which inherits their greatness, if it forget their example, may be led, through prouder eminence, to less pitied destruction.

The exaltation, the sin, and the punishment of Tyre have been recorded for us, in perhaps the most touching words ever uttered by the Prophets of Israel against the cities of the stranger. But we read them as a lovely song; and close our ears to the sternness of their warning: for the very depth of the fall of Tyre has blinded us to its reality, and we forget, as we watch the bleaching of the rocks between the sunshine and the sea, that they were once "as in Eden, the garden of God."

Her successor, like her in perfection of beauty, though less in endurance of dominion, is still left for our beholding in the final period of her decline : a ghost upon the sands of the sea, so weak,—so quiet,—so bereft of all but her loveliness, that we might well doubt, as we watched her faint reflection in the mirage of the lagoon, which was the City, and which the Shadow.

' I would endeavour to trace the lines of this image before it be for ever lost; and to record, as far as I may, the warning which seems to me to be uttered by every one of the fast-gaining waves, that beat, like passing bells, against the STONES OF VENICE.

§ II. It would be difficult to overrate the value of the lessons which might be derived from a faithful study of the history of this strange and mighty city : a history which, in spite of the labour of countless chroniclers, remains in vague and disputable outline,—barred with brightness and shade, like the far-away edge of her own ocean, where the surf and the sandbank are mingled with the sky. The inquiries in which we have to engage will hardly render this outline clearer, but their results will in some degree alter its aspect; and, so far as they bear upon it at all, they possess an interest of a far higher kind than that usually belonging to architectural investigations. I may, perhaps, in the outset, and in few words, enable the general reader to form a clearer idea of the importance of every existing expression of Venetian character through Venetian art, and of the breadth of interest which the true history of Venice embraces, than he is likely to have gleaned from the current fables of her mystery, or magnificence.

§ III. Venice is usually conceived as an oligarchy: She was so during a period less than the half of her existence, and that including the days of her decline; and it is one of the first questions needing severe examination, whether that decline was owing in any wise to the change in the form of her government, or altogether, as assuredly in great part, to changes in the character of the persons of whom it was composed.

The state of Venice existed Thirteen Hundred and Seventy-six years, from the first establishment of a consular[a] government on the island of the Rialto, to the moment when the General-in-chief of the French army of Italy pronounced the Venetian republic a thing of the past. Of this period, Two Hundred and Seventy-six years were passed in a nominal subjection to the cities of old Venetia, especially to Padua, and in an

[a] [I affectedly called it 'consular,' because the Ducal power was limited by the great council of the people, and often by two subordinate ministers. But see the clearer statement in my re-written history : " St. Mark's Rest," chap. v.]

agitated form of democracy of which the execu-
tive appears to have been entrusted to tribunes,[b]
chosen, one by the inhabitants of each of the
principal islands.   For six hundred years, during
which the power of Venice was continually on
the increase, her government was an elective
monarchy, her King or Doge possessing, in early
times at least, as much independent authority as
any other European sovereign, but an authority
gradually subjected to limitation, and shortened
almost daily of its prerogatives, while it increased
in a spectral and incapable magnificence.   The
final government of the nobles under the image
of a king lasted for five hundred years, during
which Venice reaped the fruits of her former
energies, consumed them,—and expired.

§ IV. Let the reader therefore conceive the
existence of the Venetian state as broadly
divided into two periods: the first of nine
hundred, the second of five hundred years, the
separation being marked by what was called
the " Serrar del Consiglio ; " that is to say, the
final and absolute distinction of the nobles from
the commonalty, and the establishment of the
government in their hands to the exclusion alike

[b] [There is no ' appearance' in the matter.   Each tribe or·
group of people had its own natural captain, and I don't trace
any subjection to the land cities, now.—See again the new
history.   But the main truth of the statement remains : the
government was at first democratic,—agitated, and weak.]

of the influence of the people on the one side, and the authority of the Doge on the other.

Then the first period, of nine hundred years, presents us with the most interesting spectacle of a people struggling out of anarchy into order and power; and then governed, for the most part, by the worthiest and noblest man whom they could find among them,* called their Doge or Leader, with an aristocracy gradually and resolutely forming itself around him, out of which, and at last by which, he was chosen; an aristocracy owing its origin to the accidental numbers, influence, and wealth of some among the families of the fugitives from the older Venetia, and gradually organising itself, by its unity and heroism, into a separate body.

This first period includes the Rise of Venice, her noblest achievements, and the circumstances which determined her character and position among European powers; and within its range, as might have been anticipated, we find the names of all her hero princes—of Pietro Urseolo, Ordeláfo Falier, Domenico Michieli, Sebastiano Ziani, and Enrico Dandolo.

§ v. The second period opens with a hundred and twenty years, the most eventful in the

---

* "Ha saputo trovar modo che non uno, non pochi, non molti, signoreggiano, ma molti buoni, pochi migliori, e insie-memente, *un ottimo solo.*"—*Sansovino.* Ah, well done, Venice! Wisdom this, indeed.

career of Venice—the central struggle of her life
—stained with her darkest crime, the murder
of Carrara—disturbed by her most dangerous
internal sedition, the conspiracy of Falier—oppressed by her most fatal war, the war of Chiozza
—and distinguished by the glory of her two
noblest citizens (for in this period the heroism
of her citizens replaces that of her monarchs),
Vittor Pisani and Carlo Zeno.

I date the commencement of the Fall of
Venice from the death of Carlo Zeno, 8th May,
1418; the *visible* commencement from that of
another of her noblest and wisest children, the
Doge Tomaso Mocenigo, who expired five years
later. The reign of Foscari followed, gloomy
with pestilence and war; a war in which large
acquisitions of territory were made by subtle
or fortunate policy in Lombardy, and disgrace,
significant as irreparable, sustained in the battles
on the Po at Cremona, and in the marshes of
Caravaggio. In 1454, Venice, the first of the
states of Christendom, humiliated herself to the
Turk: in the same year was established the
Inquisition of state,* and from this period her
government takes the perfidious and mysterious
form under which it is usually conceived.° In

* Daru, liv. xvi. cap. xx. We owe to this historian the
discovery of the statutes of the tribunal, and date of its establishment.

° [It has been indeed *conceived* under this form ; and was

1477, the great Turkish invasion spread terror to the shores of the lagoons; and in 1508 the league of Cambrai marks the period usually assigned as the commencement of the decline of the Venetian power; * the commercial prosperity of Venice in the close of the fifteenth century blinding her historians to the previous evidence of the diminution of her internal strength.

§ vi. Now there is apparently a significative coincidence between the establishment of the aristocratic and oligarchical powers, and the diminution of the prosperity of the state. But this is the very question at issue; and it appears to me quite undetermined by any historian, or determined by each in accordance with his own prejudices. It is a triple question: first, whether the oligarchy established by the efforts of individual ambition was the cause, in its subsequent operation, of the fall of Venice; or (secondly) whether the establishment of the oligarchy itself be not the sign and evidence, rather than the cause, of national enervation; or (lastly) whether, as I rather think, the history of Venice might not be written almost without reference to the

assuredly in many respects 'mysterious,' and in some acts, 'perfidious.' I believe it merits the title, in the essential spirit of its government, as much as " perfide Albion."]

* Ominously signified by their humiliation to the Papal power (as before to the Turkish) in 1509, and their abandonment of their right of appointing the clergy of their territories.

construction of her senate, or the prerogatives of her Doge. It is the history of a people eminently at unity in itself, descendants of Roman race, long disciplined by adversity, and compelled by its position either to live nobly or to perish :—for a thousand years they fought for life ; for three hundred they invited death : their battle was rewarded, and their call was heard.

§ VII. Throughout her career, the victories of Venice, and, at many periods of it, her safety, were purchased by individual heroism ; and the man who exalted or saved her was sometimes (oftenest) her king, sometimes her noble, sometimes a citizen. To him no matter, nor to her : the real question is, not so much what names they bore, or with what powers they were entrusted, as how they were trained; how they were made masters of themselves, servants of their country, patient of distress, impatient of dishonour ; and what was the true reason of the change from the time when she could find saviours among those whom she had cast into prison, to that when the voices of her own children commanded her to sign covenant with Death.*

§ VIII. On this collateral question I wish the reader's mind to be fixed, throughout all our subsequent inquiries. It will give double

* The senate voted the abdication of their authority by a majority of 512 to 14.—Alison, ch. xxiii.

interest to every detail: nor will the interest be
profitless; for the evidence which I shall be able
to deduce from the arts of Venice will be both
frequent and irrefragable, that the decline of her
political prosperity was exactly coincident with
that of domestic and individual religion.

I say domestic and individual; for—and this
is the second point which I wish the reader to
keep in mind—the most curious phenomenon in
all Venetian history is the vitality of religion
in private life, and its deadness in public policy.
Amidst the enthusiasm, chivalry, or fanaticism
of the other states of Europe, Venice stands, from
first to last, like a masked statue; her coldness impenetrable; her exertion only aroused by
the touch of a secret spring. That spring was
her commercial interest,—this the one motive of
all her important political acts, or enduring
national animosities. She could forgive insults
to her honour, but never rivalship in her com-
merce; she calculated the glory of her conquests
by their value, and estimated their justice by
their facility. The fame of success remains,
when the motives of attempt are forgotten; and
the casual reader of her history may perhaps be
surprised to be reminded, that the expedition
which was commanded by the noblest of her
princes, and whose results added most to her
military glory, was one in which, while all
Europe around her was wasted by the fire of its

devotion, she first calculated the highest price she could exact from its piety for the armament she furnished, and then, for the advancement of her own private interests, at once broke her faith * and betrayed her religion.

§ IX. And yet, in the midst of this national criminality, we shall be struck again and again by the evidences of the most noble individual feeling. The tears of Dandolo were not shed in hypocrisy, though they could not blind him to the importance of the conquest of Zara. The habit of assigning to religion a direct influence over all *his own* actions, and all the affairs of *his own* daily life, is remarkable in every great Venetian during the times of the prosperity of the state; nor are instances wanting in which the private feeling of the citizens reaches the sphere of their policy, and even becomes the guide of its course where the scales of expediency are doubtfully balanced. I sincerely trust that the inquirer would be disappointed who should endeavour to trace any more immediate reasons for their adoption of the cause of Alexander III. against Barbarossa, than the piety which was excited by the character of their suppliant, and the noble pride which was provoked by the insolence of the emperor. But the heart of Venice is shown only in her hastiest

* By directing the arms of the Crusaders against a Christian prince.—Daru, liv. iv. ch. iv., viii.

councils; [d] her worldly spirit recovers the ascendency whenever she has time to calculate the probabilities of advantage, or when they are sufficiently distinct to need no calculation; and the entire subjection of private piety to national policy is not only remarkable throughout the almost endless series of treacheries and tyrannies by which her empire was enlarged and maintained, but symbolised by a very singular circumstance in the building of the city itself. I am aware of no other city of Europe in which its cathedral was not the principal feature. But the principal Church in Venice was the chapel attached to the palace of her prince, and called the "Chiesa Ducale." The patriarchal church,* inconsiderable in size and mean in decoration, stands on the outermost islet of the Venetian group, and its name, as well as its site, are probably unknown to the greater number of travellers passing hastily through the city. Nor is it less worthy of remark, that the two most important temples of Venice, next to the ducal chapel, owe their size and magnificence, not to national efforts, but to the energy of the

---

[d] [Yes: that is so,—but it *is* her heart, which was the main gist of the matter,—fool that I was not to understand! Venice is superficially and apparently commercial;—at heart passionately heroic and religious; precisely the reverse of modern England, who is superficially and apparently religious; and at heart, entirely infidel, cowardly, and dishonest.]

* " San Pietro di Castello."

Franciscan and Dominican monks, supported by the vast organisation of those great societies on the mainland of Italy, and countenanced by the most pious, and perhaps also, in his generation, the most wise, of all the princes of Venice,* who now rests beneath the roof of one of those very temples, and whose life is not satirized by the images of the Virtues which a Tuscan sculptor has placed around his tomb.

§ x. There are, therefore, two strange and solemn lights in which we have to regard almost every scene in the fitful history of the Rivo Alto. We find, on the one hand, a deep and constant tone of individual religion character-ising the lives of the citizens of Venice in her greatness; we find this spirit influencing them in all the familiar and immediate concerns of life, giving a peculiar dignity to the conduct even of their commercial transactions, and confessed by them with a simplicity of faith that may well put to shame the hesitation with which a man of the world at present admits (even if it be so in reality) that religious feeling has any influence over the minor branches of his conduct. And we find as the natural consequence of all this, a healthy serenity of mind, and energy of will, expressed in all their actions, and a habit of

---

* Tomaso Mocenigo, above named, § v.—[His tomb is in the northern aisle of S. Giovanni e Paolo. See p. 41, and vol. ii. p. 101.]

heroism which never fails them, even when the immediate motive of action ceased to be praise-worthy. With the fulness of this spirit the prosperity of the state is exactly correspondent, and with its failure her decline, and that with a closeness and precision which it will be one of the collateral objects of the following essay to demonstrate from such accidental evidence as the field of its inquiry presents. And, thus far, all is natural and simple. But the stopping short of this religious faith when it appears likely to influence national action, correspondent as it is, and that most strikingly, with several character-istics of the temper of our present English legislature, is a subject, morally and politically, of the most curious interest and complicated difficulty; one, however, which the range of my present inquiry will not permit me to approach, and for the treatment of which I must be content to furnish materials in the light I may be able to throw upon the private tendencies of the Venetian character.

§ XI. There is, however, another most inte-resting feature in the policy of Venice which will be often brought before us; and which a Romanist would gladly assign as the reason of its irreligion; namely, the magnificent and suc-cessful struggle which she maintained against the temporal authority of the Church of Rome. It is true that, in a rapid survey of her career,

the eye is at first arrested by the strange drama
to which I have already alluded, closed by that
ever memorable scene in the portico of St.
Mark's,* the central expression in most men's
thoughts of the unendurable elevation of the
pontifical power ;ᵉ it is true that the proudest
thoughts of Venice, as well as the insignia of her
prince, and the form of her chief festival, recorded
the service thus rendered to the Roman Church.
But the enduring sentiment of years more than
balanced the enthusiasm of a moment; and the
bull of Clement V., which excommunicated the
Venetians and their Doge, likening them to
Dathan, Abiram, Absalom, and Lucifer, is a
stronger evidence of the great tendencies of the
Venetian government than the umbrella of the

> *   "In that temple porch,
> (The brass is gone, the porphyry remains,)
> Did BARBAROSSA fling his mantle off,
> And kneeling, on his neck receive the foot
> Of the proud Pontiff—thus at last consoled
> For flight, disguise, and many an anguish shake
> On his stone pillow."

I need hardly say whence the lines are taken : Roger's
' Italy' has, I believe, now a place in the best beloved com-
partment of all libraries, and will never be removed from it.
There is more true expression of the spirit of Venice in the
passages devoted to her in that poem, than in all else that has
been written of her.

*[Most men being geese, in everything they think and say
of all powers above them. See true account of this scene to
ve given in ' St. Mark's Rest.']

Doge, or the ring of the Adriatic. The humiliation of Francesco Dandolo blotted out the shame
of Barbarossa, and the total exclusion of eccle-
siastics from all share in the councils of Venice
became an enduring mark of her knowledge of
the spirit of the Church of Rome, and of her
defiance of it.

To this exclusion of Papal influence from her
councils, the Romanist will attribute their irreligion, and the Protestant their success.* The
first may be silenced by a reference to the character of the policy of the Vatican itself; and
the second by his own shame, when he reflects
that the English legislature sacrificed their principles to expose themselves to the very danger
which the Venetian senate sacrificed theirs to
avoid.

§ XII. One more circumstance remains to be
noted respecting the Venetian government, the
singular unity of the families composing it,—
unity far from sincere or perfect, but still admirable when contrasted with the fiery feuds, the
almost daily revolutions, the restless successions
of families and parties in power, which fill the
annals of the other states of Italy. That rivalship should sometimes be ended by the dagger, or
enmity conducted to its ends under the mask of
law, could not but be anticipated where the fierce

* At least, such success as they had. Vide Appendix 5 (old
edition) : " The Papal Power in Venice."

Italian spirit was subjected to so severe a restraint: it is much that jealousy appears usually unmingled with illegitimate ambition, and that, for every instance in which private passion sought its gratification through public danger, there are a thousand in which it was sacrificed to the public advantage. Venice may well call upon us to note with reverence, that of all the towers which are still seen rising like a branchless forest from her islands, there is but one whose office was other than that of summoning to prayer, and that one was a watch-tower only :[f] from first to last, while the palaces of the other cities of Italy were lifted into sullen fortitudes of rampart, and fringed with forked battlements for the javelin and the bow, the sands of Venice never sank under the weight of a war tower, and her roof terraces were wreathed with Arabian imagery, of golden globes suspended on the leaves of lilies.[*]

§ xiii. These, then, appear to me to be the points of chief general interest in the character and fate of the Venetian people. I would next endeavour to give the reader some idea of the

---

[f] [Thus literally was fulfilled the promise to St. Mark,—Pax tibi Marce.]

[*] The inconsiderable fortifications of the arsenal are no exception to this statement, as far as it regards the city itself. They are little more than a semblance of precaution against the attack of a foreign enemy.

manner in which the testimony of Art bears upon these questions, and of the aspect which the arts themselves assume when they are regarded in their true connection with the history of the state :—

First, receive the witness of Painting.

It will be remembered that I put the commencement of the Fall of Venice as far back as 1418.

Now, John Bellini was born in 1423, and Titian in 1480. John Bellini, and his brother Gentile, two years older than he, close the line of the sacred painters of Venice. But the most solemn spirit of religious faith animates their works to the last. There is no religion in any work of Titian's : [g] there is not even the smallest evidence of religious temper or sympathies either in himself, or in those for whom he painted. His larger sacred subjects are merely themes for the exhibition of pictorial rhetoric,—composition and colour. His minor works are generally made subordinate to purposes of portraiture. The Madonna in the church of the Frari is a mere lay figure, introduced to form a link of connection between the portraits of various members of the Pesaro family who surround her.

Now this is not merely because John Bellini

[g] [These two paragraphs, xiii. and xiv., are as true and sound as they are audacious. I am very proud of them, on re-reading.]

was a religious man and Titian was not. Titian
and Bellini are each true representatives of the
school of painters contemporary with them ; and'
the difference in their artistic feeling is a consequence not so much of difference in their own
natural characters as in their early education :
Bellini was brought up in faith ; Titian in formalism. Between the years of their births the
vital religion of Venice had expired.

§ XIV. The *vital* religion, observe, not the
formal. Outward observance was as strict as
ever ; and Doge and senator still were painted,
in almost every important instance, kneeling
before the Madonna or St. Mark ; a confession of
faith made universal by the pure gold of the
Venetian sequin. But observe the great picture
of Titian's, in the Ducal Palace, of the Doge
Antonio Grimani kneeling before Faith : there is
a curious lesson in it. The figure of Faith is
a coarse portrait of one of Titian's least graceful
female models : Faith had become carnal. The
eye is first caught by the flash of the Doge's
armour : the heart of Venice was in her wars,
not in her worship.

The mind of Tintoret, incomparably more deep
and serious than that of Titian, casts the solem-
nity of its own tone over the sacred subjects
which it approaches, and sometimes forgets itself into devotion ; but the principle of treatment
is altogether the same as Titian's : absolute

subordination of the religious subject to purposes of decoration or portraiture.

The evidence might be accumulated a thousandfold from the works of Veronese, and of every succeeding painter,—that the fifteenth century had taken away the religious heart of Venice.

§ xv. Such is the evidence of Painting. To collect that of Architecture will be our task through many a page to come ; but I must here give a general idea of its heads.

Philippe de Commynes, writing of his entry into Venice in 1495, says,—

"Chascun me feit seoir au meillieu de ces deux ambassadeurs qui est l'honneur d'Italie que d'estre au meillieu ; et me menerent au long de la grant rue, qu'ilz appellent le Canal Grant, et est bien large. Les gallees y passent à travers, et y ay veu navire de quatre cens tonneaux ou plus pres des maisons : et est la plus belle rue que je croy qui soit en tout le monde, et la mieulx maisonnee, et va le long de la ville. Les maisons sont fort grandes et haultes, et de bonne pierre, et les anciennes toutes painctes ; les aultres faictes depuis cent ans : toutes ont le devant de marbre blanc, qui leur vient d'Istrie, à cent mils de là, et encores maincte grant piece de porphire et de sarpentine sur le devant. . . . . C'est la plus triumphante cité que j'aye jamais veue et qui plus faict d'honneur à ambassadeurs et estrangiers, et

qui plus saigement se gouverne, et où le service
de Dieu est le plus sollempnellement faict :
et encores qu'il y peust bien avoir d'aultres
faultes si je croy que Dieu les a en ayde
pour la reverence qu'ilz portent au service
de l'Eglise." *

§ XVI. This passage is of peculiar interest, for
two reasons. Observe, first, the impression of
Commynes respecting the religion of Venice: of
which, as I have above said, the forms still remained with some glimmering of life in them,
and were the evidence of what the real life had
been in former times. But observe, secondly,
the impression instantly made on Commynes'
mind by the distinction between the older palaces
and those built "within this last hundred years;
which all have their fronts of white marble
brought from Istria, a hundred miles away, and
besides, many a large piece of porphyry and
serpentine upon their fronts."

On the opposite page I have given two of the
ornaments of the palaces which so struck the
French ambassador.† He was right in his notice
of the distinction. There had indeed come a
change over Venetian architecture in the fifteenth
century; and a change of some importance to
us moderns: we English owe to it our St. Paul's
Cathedral, and Europe in general owes to it the

* Mémoires de Commynes, liv. vii. ch. xviii.
† Appendix 6 (old edition): " Renaissance Ornaments."

utter degradation or destruction of her schools
of architecture, never since revived. But that
the reader may understand this, it is necessary
that he should have some general idea of the
connection of the architecture of Venice with
that of the rest of Europe, from its origin
forwards.

§ XVII. All European architecture, bad and
good, old and new, is derived from Greece
through Rome, and coloured and perfected from
the East. The history of architecture is nothing
but the tracing of the various modes and directions of this derivation. Understand this, once
for all: if you hold fast this great connecting
clue, you may string all the types of successive
architectural invention upon it like so many
beads. The Doric and the Corinthian orders are
the roots, the one of all Romanesque, massy-
capitaled buildings—Norman, Lombard, Byzantine, and what else you can name of the kind;
and the Corinthian of all Gothic, Early English,
French, German, and Tuscan. Now observe:
those old Greeks gave the shaft; Rome gave the
arch; the Arabs pointed and foliated the arch.
The shaft and arch, the framework and strength
of architecture, are from the race of Japheth:
the spirituality and sanctity of it from Ishmael,
Abraham, and Shem.

§ XVIII. There is a high probability that the
Greek received his shaft system from Egypt;

but I do not care to keep this earlier derivation
in the mind of the reader. It is only necessary
that he should be able to refer to a fixed point
of origin, when the form of the shaft was first
perfected. But it may be incidentally observed,
that if the Greeks did indeed receive their Doric
from Egypt, then the three families of the earth
have each contributed their part to its noblest
architecture : and Ham, the servant of the others,
furnishes the sustaining or bearing member, the
shaft; Japheth the arch; Shem the spiritualisation of both.

§ XIX. I have said that the two orders, Doric
and Corinthian, are the roots of all European
architecture. You have, perhaps, heard of five
orders: but there are only two real orders; and
there never can be any more until doomsday.
On one of these orders the ornament is convex:
those are Doric, Norman, and what else you
recollect of the kind. The transitional form, in
which the ornamental line is straight, is the
centre or root of both. All other orders are
varieties of these, or phantasms and grotesques,
altogether indefinite in number and species.*

§ XX. This Greek architecture, then, with its
two orders, was clumsily copied and varied by
the Romans with no particular result, until they
began to bring the arch into extensive practical

---

* Appendix 7 (old edition) : " Varieties of the Orders."

service; except only that the Doric capital was spoiled in endeavours to mend it, and the Corinthian much varied and enriched with fanciful, and often very beautiful imagery. And in this state of things came Christianity: seized upon the arch as her own: decorated it, and delighted in it: invented a new Doric capital to replace the spoiled Roman one: and all over the Roman empire set to work, with such materials as were nearest at hand, to express and adorn herself as best she could. This Roman Christian architecture is the exact expression of the Christianity of the time, very fervid and beautiful—but very imperfect; in many respects ignorant, and yet radiant with a strong, childish light of imagination, which flames up under Constantine, illumines all the shores of the Bosphorus and the Ægean and the Adriatic Sea, and then gradually, as the people give themselves up to idolatry, becomes corpse-light. The architecture, like the religion it expressed, sinks into a settled form— a strange, gilded, and embalmed repose; and so would have remained for ever,—so *does* remain, where its languor has been undisturbed.* But rough wakening was ordained for it.

§ XXI. This Christian art of the declining

---

* The reader will find the *weak* points of Byzantine architecture shrewdly seized, and exquisitely sketched, in the opening chapter of the most delightful book of travels I ever opened,—Curzon's ' Monasteries of the Levant.'

empire is divided into two great branches,
western and eastern; one centred at Rome, the
other at Byzantium, of which the one is the early
Christian Romanesque, properly so called, and
the other, carried to higher imaginative perfection
by Greek workmen, is distinguished from it as
Byzantine. But I wish the reader, for the present, to class these two branches of art together
in his mind,[h] they being, in points of main importance, the same; that is to say, both of them
a true continuance and sequence of the art of
old Rome .itself, flowing uninterruptedly down
from the fountain-head, and entrusted always to
the best workmen who could be found—Latins
in Italy and Greeks in Greece; and thus both
branches may be ranged under the general term
of Christian Romanesque, an architecture which
had lost the refinement of Pagan art in the
degradation of the Empire, but which was ele-

[h] [This was a great error of mine, in endeavour for simplicity.
The Greek school at Byzantium is pure Greek in decline; but
that which passed through the Roman mind, and formed
Roman and Romanesque architecture in North Europe, was
sensualized and brutalized into forms which developed the
Northern fleshly or naturalist instincts. Taken up by Niccolo
Pisano, it superseded the old Greek, under Cimabue. For full
statement of this, see the ' Laws of Fésole; ' and at present,
to set these pages right, omit from " But I wish " as far as
' brighter forms," and for the second sentence of the twenty-
second paragraph, read, " While in Rome, this corruptly
enriched Roman art, and at Byzantium, this religiously-pining
Greek art, were practised in all their refinements."]

vated by Christianity to higher aims, and by the fancy of the Greek workmen endowed with brighter forms. And this art the reader may conceive as extending in its various branches over all the central provinces of the empire, taking aspects more or less refined, according to its proximity to the seats of government; dependent for all its power on the vigour and freshness of the religion which animated it; and as that vigour and purity departed, losing its own vitality, and sinking into nerveless rest, not deprived of its beauty, but benumbed, and incapable of advance or change.

§ XXII. Meantime there had been preparation for its renewal. While in Rome and Constantinople, and in the districts under their immediate influence, this Roman art of pure descent was practised in all its refinement, an impure form of it—a patois of Romanesque—was carried by inferior workmen into distant provinces; and still ruder imitations of this patois were executed by the barbarous nations on the skirts of the empire. But these barbarous nations were in the strength of their youth; and while, in the centre of Europe, a refined and purely descended art was sinking into graceful formalism, on its confines a barbarous and borrowed art was organising itself into strength and consistency. The reader must therefore consider the history of the work of the period as broadly

divided into two great heads : the one embracing
the elaborately languid succession of the Christian art of Rome ; and the other, the imitations
of it executed by nations in every conceivable
phase of early organisation, on the edges of the
Empire, or included in its now merely nominal
extent.

§ XXIII. Some of the barbaric nations were,
of course, not susceptible of this influence ; and,
when they burst over the Alps, appear like the
Huns, as scourges only, or mix, as the Ostrogoths,
with the enervated Italians, and give physical
strength to the mass with which they mingle,
without materially affecting its intellectual character. But others, both south and north of the
Empire, had felt its influence, back to the beach
of the Indian Ocean on the one hand, and to
the ice creeks of the North Sea on the other.
On the north and west the influence was of the
Latins ; on the south and east, of the Greeks.
Two nations, pre-eminent above all the rest,
represent to us the force of derived mind on
either side. As the central power is eclipsed,
the orbs of reflected light gather into their
fulness ; and when sensuality and idolatry had
done their work, and the religion of the Empire
was laid asleep in a glittering sepulchre, the
living light rose upon both horizons, and the
fierce swords of the Lombard and Arab were
shaken over its golden paralysis.

§ XXIV. The work of the Lombard was to give hardihood and system to the enervated body and enfeebled mind of Christendom; that of the Arab was to punish idolatry, and to proclaim spirituality of worship. The Lombard covered every church which he built with the sculptured representations of bodily exercises—hunting and war.* The Arab banished all imagination of creature form from his temples, and proclaimed from their minarets, "There is no god but God." Opposite in their character and mission, alike in their magnificence of energy, they came from the North and from the South, the glacier torrent and the lava stream: they met and contended over the wreck of the Roman empire; and the very centre of the struggle, the point of pause of both, the dead water of the opposite eddies, charged with embayed fragments of the Roman wreck, is VENICE.

The Ducal Palace of Venice contains the three elements in exactly equal proportions—the Roman, Lombard, and Arab. It is the central building of the world.

§ XXV. The reader will now begin to understand something of the importance of the study of the edifices of a city which concludes, within the circuit of some seven or eight miles, the field of contest between the three pre-eminent

* Appendix 8 (old edition) : "The Northern Energy."

architectures of the world :—each architecture expressing a condition of religion; each an erroneous condition, yet necessary to the correction of the others, and corrected by them.

§ xxvi. It will be part of my endeavour, in the following work, to mark the various modes in which the northern and southern architectures were developed from the Roman: here I must pause only to name the distinguishing characteristics of the great families. The Christian Roman and Byzantine work is round-arched, with single and well-proportioned shafts; capitals imitated from classical Roman;[1] mouldings more or less so; and large surfaces of walls entirely covered with imagery, mosaic, and painting, whether of Scripture history or of sacred symbols.

The Arab school is at first the same in its principal features, the Byzantine workmen being employed by the caliphs; but the Arab rapidly introduces characters half Persepolitan, half Egyptian, into the shafts and capitals: in his intense love of excitement he points the arch and writhes it into extravagant foliations; he banishes the animal imagery, and invents an

---

[1] [Classical Greek, it should have been. I did not at this time myself know the difference between Roman and Greek treatment of acanthus. The rest of the chapter is now perfectly right, except in the slip pointed out at page 40.]

ornamentation of his own (called Arabesque) to replace it: this not being adapted for covering large surfaces, he concentrates it on features of interest, and bars his surfaces with horizontal lines of colour, the expression of the level of the Desert. He retains the dome, and adds the minaret. All is done with exquisite refinement.

§ XXVII. The changes effected by the Lombard are more curious still, for they are in the anatomy of the building, more than its decoration. The Lombard architecture represents, as I said, the whole of that of the northern barbaric nations. And this I believe was, at first, an imitation in wood of the Christian Roman churches or basilicas. Without staying to examine the whole structure of a basilica, the reader will easily understand this much of it: that it had a nave and two aisles, the nave much higher than the aisles; that the nave was separated from the aisles by rows of shafts, which supported, above, large spaces of flat or dead wall, rising above the aisles, and forming the upper part of the nave, now called the clerestory, which had a gabled wooden roof.

The high dead walls were, in Roman work, built of stone; but in the wooden work of the North, they must necessarily have been made of horizontal boards or timbers attached to uprights on the top of the nave pillars, which were

themselves also of wood.* Now these uprights
were necessarily thicker than the rest of the
timbers, and formed vertical square pilasters
above the nave piers. As Christianity extended
and civilisation increased, these wooden structures
were changed into stone: but they were literally
petrified, retaining the form which had been
made necessary by their being of wood. The
upright pilaster above the nave pier remains in
the stone edifice, and is the first form of the
great distinctive feature of Northern architecture
—the vaulting shaft. In that form the Lombards brought it into Italy in the seventeenth
century, and it remains to this day in St.
Ambrogio of Milan, and St. Michele of Pavia.

§ XXVIII. When the vaulting shaft was introduced in the clerestory walls, additional members
were added for its support to the nave piers.
Perhaps two or three pine trunks, used for a
single pillar, gave the first idea of the grouped
shaft. Be that as it may, the arrangement of
the nave pier in the form of a cross accompanies
the superimposition of the vaulting shaft; together with correspondent grouping of minor
shafts in doorways and apertures of windows.
Thus, the whole body of the Northern architecture, represented by that of the Lombards, may
be described as rough but majestic work, round

* Appendix 9 (old edition): "Wooden Churches of the
North."

arched, with grouped shafts, added vaulting shafts, and endless imagery of active life and fantastic superstitions.

§ xxix. The glacier stream of the Lombards, and the following one of the Normans, left their erratic blocks wherever they had flowed; but without influencing, I think, the Southern nations beyond the sphere of their own presence. But the lava stream of the Arab, even after it ceased to flow, warmed the whole of the Northern air; and the history of Gothic architecture is the history of the refinement and spiritualisation of Northern work under its influence. The noblest buildings of the world, the Pisan-Romanesque, Tuscan (Giottesque) Gothic, and Veronese Gothic, are those of the Lombard schools themselves, under its close and direct influence; the various Gothics of the North are the original forms of the architecture which the Lombards brought into Italy, changing under the less direct influence of the Arab.

§ xxx. Understanding this much of the formation of the great European styles, we shall have no difficulty in tracing the succession of architectures in Venice herself. From what I said of the central character of Venetian art, the reader is not, of course, to conclude that the Roman, Northern, and Arabian elements met together and contended for the mastery at the same period. The earliest element was the pure

Christian Roman; but few, if any, remains of this art exist at Venice; for the present city was in the earliest times only one of many settlements formed on the chain of marshy islands which extend from the mouths of the Isonzo to those of the Adige, and it was not until the beginning of the ninth century that it became the seat of government; while the cathedral of Torcello, though Christian Roman in general form, was rebuilt in the eleventh century, and shows evidence of Byzantine workmanship in many of its details. This cathedral however, with the church of Santa Fosca at Torcello, San Giacomo di Rialto at Venice, and the crypt of St. Mark's, form a distinct group of building, in which the Byzantine influence is exceedingly slight; and which is probably very sufficiently representative of the earliest architecture on the islands.

§ xxxi. The ducal residence was removed to Venice in 809, and the body of St. Mark was brought from Alexandria twenty years later. The first church of St. Mark's was, doubtless, built in imitation of that destroyed at Alexandria, and from which the relics of the Saint had been obtained. During the ninth, tenth, and eleventh centuries, the architecture of Venice seems to have been formed on the same model, and is almost identical with that of Cairo under the caliphs,* it being quite immaterial whether

* Appendix 10 (old edition) : " Church of Alexandria."

the reader chooses to call both Byzantine or both Arabic; the workmen being certainly Byzantine, but forced to the invention of new forms by their Arabian masters, and bringing these forms into use in whatever other parts of the world they were employed.

To this first manner of Venetian Architecture, together with such vestiges as remain of the Christian Roman, I shall devote the first division of the following inquiry. The examples remaining of it consist of three noble churches (those of Torcello, Murano, and the greater part of St. Mark's), and about ten or twelve fragments of palaces.

§ XXXII. To this style succeeds a transitional one of a character much more distinctly Arabian : the shafts become more slender, and the arches consistently pointed, instead of round; certain other changes, not to be enumerated in a sentence, taking place in the capitals and mouldings. This style is almost exclusively secular. It was natural for the Venetians to imitate the beautiful details of the Arabian dwelling-house, while they would with reluctance adopt those of the mosque for Christian churches.

I have not succeeded in fixing limiting dates for this style. It appears in part contemporary with the Byzantine manner, but outlives it. Its position is, however, fixed by the central date, 1180, that of the elevation of the granite shafts of the Piazzetta, whose capitals are the two most important pieces of detail in this transitional style in Venice. Examples of its application to domestic buildings exist in almost every street of the city, and will form the subject of the second division of the following essay.

§ XXXIII. The Venetians were always ready to receive lessons in art from their enemies (else had there been no Arab work in Venice). But their especial dread and hatred of the Lombards appear to have long prevented them from receiving the influence of the art which that people had introduced on the mainland of Italy. Nevertheless, during the practice of the two styles above distinguished, a peculiar and very primitive condition of pointed Gothic had arisen in ecclesiastical architecture. It appears to be a feeble reflection of the Lombard-Arab forms, which were attaining perfection upon the Continent, and would probably, if left to itself, have been soon merged in the Venetian-Arab school, with which it had from the first so close a fellowship, that it will be found difficult to distinguish the Arabian ogives from those which seem to have been built under this early Gothic influence. The churches of San Giacopo dell' Orio, San Giovanni in Bragora, the Carmine, and one or two more, furnish the only important examples of it. But, in the thirteenth century, the Franciscans and Dominicans introduced from

the Continent their morality and their architecture, already a distinct Gothic, curiously
developed from Lombardic and Northern (German?) forms; and the influence of the principles
exhibited in the vast churches of St. Paul and
the Frari began rapidly to affect the Venetian-
Arab school. Still the two systems never became
united; the Venetian policy repressed the
power of the Church, and the Venetian artists
resisted its example; and thenceforward the
architecture of the city becomes divided into
ecclesiastical and civil: the one an ungraceful
yet powerful form of the Western Gothic,
common to the whole peninsula, and only showing Venetian sympathies in the adoption of
certain characteristic mouldings; the other a
rich, luxuriant, and entirely original Gothic,
formed from the Venetian-Arab by the influence
of the Dominican and Franciscan architecture,
and especially by the engrafting upon the Arab
forms of the most novel feature of the Franciscan
work, its traceries. These various forms of
Gothic, the *distinctive* architecture of Venice
chiefly represented by the churches of St. John
and Paul, the Frari and San Stefano, on the
ecclesiastical side, and by the Ducal Palace, and
the other principal Gothic palaces, on the secular
side, will be the subject of the third division of
the essay.

§ XXXIV. Now observe. The traditional (or

especially Arabic) style of the Venetian work
is centralised by the date 1180, and is transformed gradually into the Gothic, which extends
in its purity from the middle of the thirteenth
to the beginning of the fifteenth century ; that
is to say, over the precise period which I have
described as the central epoch of the life of
Venice. I dated her decline from the year 1418 ;
Foscari became doge five years later, and in his
reign the first marked signs appear in architecture of that mighty change which Philippe
de Commynes notices as above, the change to
which London owes St. Paul's, Rome St. Peter's,
Venice and Vicenza the edifices commonly supposed to be their noblest, and Europe in general
the degradation of every art she has since
practised.

§ xxxv. This change appears first in a loss
of truth and vitality in existing architecture
all over the world. (Compare 'Seven Lamps,'
chap. ii.) All the Gothics in existence, southern
or northern, were corrupted at once : the German
and French lost themselves in every species of
extravagance; the English Gothic was confined,
in its insanity, by a strait-waistcoat of perpen-
dicular lines ; the Italian effloresced on the
mainland into the meaningless ornamentation
of the Certosa of Pavia and the Cathedral of
Como (a style sometimes ignorantly called
Italian Gothic), and at Venice into the insipid

confusion of the Porta della Carta and wild crockets of St. Mark's. This corruption of all architecture, especially ecclesiastical, corresponded with, and marked, the state of religion over all Europe,—the peculiar degradation of the Romanist superstition, and of public morality in consequence, which brought about the Reformation.

§ XXXVI. Against the corrupted papacy arose two great divisions of adversaries, Protestants in Germany and England, Rationalists in France and Italy; the one requiring the purification of religion, the other its destruction. The Protestant kept the religion, but cast aside the heresies of Rome, and with them her arts, by which last rejection he injured his own character, cramped his intellect in refusing to it one of its noblest exercises, and materially diminished his influence. It may be a serious question how far the Pausing of the Reformation has been a consequence of this error.

The Rationalist kept the arts and cast aside the religion. This rationalistic art is the art commonly called Renaissance, marked by a return to pagan systems, not to adopt them and hallow them for Christianity, but to rank itself under them as an imitator and pupil. In Painting it is headed by Giulio Romano and Nicolo Poussin; in Architecture, by Sansovino and Palladio.

§ XXXVII. Instant degradation followed in every direction,—a flood of folly and hypocrisy. Mythologies, ill understood at first, then perverted into feeble sensualities, take the place of the representations of Christian subjects, which had become blasphemous under the treatment of men like the Caracci. Gods without power, satyrs without rusticity, nymphs without innocence, men without humanity, gather into idiot groups upon the polluted canvas, and scenic affectations encumber the streets with preposterous marble. Lower and lower declines the level of abused intellect; the base school of landscape* gradually usurps the place of the historical painting, which had sunk into prurient pedantry,—the Alsatian sublimities of Salvator, the confectionery idealities of Claude, the dull manufacture of Gaspar and Canaletto, south of the Alps, and on the north the patient devotion of besotted lives to delineation of bricks and fogs, fat cattle and ditchwater. And thus, Christianity and morality, courage, and intellect, and art, all crumbling together into one wreck, we are hurried on to the fall of Italy, the revolution in France, and the condition of art in England (saved by her Protestantism from severer penalty) in the time of George II.

§ XXXVIII. I have not written in vain if I

---

* Appendix 11 (old edition) : " Renaissance Landscape."

have heretofore done anything towards dimi-
nishing the reputation of the Renaissance landscape painting. But the harm which has been
done by Claude and the Poussins is as nothing
when compared to the mischief effected by
Palladio, Scamozzi, and Sansovino. Claude and
the Poussins were weak men, and have had no
serious influence on the general mind. There is
little harm in their works being purchased at
high prices: their real influence is very slight,
and they may be left without grave indignation
to their poor mission of furnishing drawing-
rooms and assisting stranded conversation. Not
so the Renaissance architecture. Raised at once
into all the magnificence of which it was capable
by Michael Angelo, then taken up by men of
real intellect and imagination, such as Scamozzi,
Sansovino, Inigo Jones, and Wren, it is impossible
to estimate the extent of its influence on the
European mind; and that the more, because few
persons are concerned with painting, and, of
those few, the larger number regard it with
slight attention; but all men are concerned with
architecture, and have at some time of their
lives serious business with it. It does not much
matter that an individual loses two or three
hundred pounds in buying a bad picture, but
it is to be regretted that a nation should lose
two or three hundred thousand in raising a
ridiculous building. Nor is it merely wasted

wealth or distempered conception which we
have to regret in this Renaissance architecture;
but we shall find in it partly the root, partly the
expression, of certain dominant evils of modern
times—over-sophistication and ignorant classicalism; the one destroying the healthfulness of
general society, the other rendering our schools
and universities useless to a large number of
the men who pass through them.

Now Venice, as she was once the most religious, was in her fall the most corrupt, of
European states; and she was in her strength
the centre[k] of the pure currents of Christian
architecture, so she is in her decline the source
of the Renaissance. It was the originality and
splendour of the palaces of Vicenza and Venice
which gave this school its eminence in the eyes
of Europe; and the dying city, magnificent in
her dissipation, and graceful in her follies, obtained wider worship in her decrepitude than
in her youth, and sank from the midst of her
admirers into the grave.

§ XXXIX. It is in Venice, therefore, and in
Venice only, that effectual blows can be struck
at this pestilent art of the Renaissance. Destroy

---

[k] [I am ashamed of having been so entrapped by my
own metaphor. Look back to § 24. She was the *centre*
of Christian art only as the place of slack water between
contending currents. I confuse that notion here, with the
central power of a fountain in a pool.]

its claims to admiration there, and it can assert them nowhere else. This, therefore, will be the final purpose of the following essay. I shall not devote a fourth section to Palladio, nor weary the reader with successive chapters of vituperation; but I shall, in my account of the earlier architecture, compare the forms of all its leading features with those into which they were corrupted by the Classicalists; and pause, in the close, on the edge of the precipice of decline, so soon as I have made its depth discernible. In doing this I shall depend upon two distinct kinds of evidence :—the first, the testimony borne by particular incidents and facts to a want of thought or of feeling in the builders; from which we may conclude that their architecture must be bad :—the second, the sense, which I doubt not I shall be able to excite in the reader, of a systematic ugliness in the architecture itself. Of the first kind of testimony I shall here give two instances, which may be immediately useful in fixing in the reader's mind the epoch above indicated for the commencement of decline.

§ XL. I must again refer to the importance which I have above attached to the death of Carlo Zeno and the Doge Tomaso Mocenigo. The tomb of that doge is, as I said, wrought by a Florentine; but it is of the same general type and feeling as all the Venetian tombs of the period, and it is one of the last which retains it. The

classical element enters largely into its details,
but the feeling of the whole is as yet unaffected.
Like all the lovely tombs of Venice and Verona,
it is a sarcophagus with a recumbent figure
above, and this figure is a faithful but tender
portrait, wrought as far as it can be without
painfulness, of the doge as he lay in death. He
wears his ducal robe and bonnet—his head is
laid slightly aside upon his pillow—his hands are
simply crossed as they fall. The face is emaciated,
the features large, but so pure and lordly in their
natural chiselling, that they must have looked
like marble even in their animation. They are
deeply worn away by thought and death; the
veins on the temples branched and starting; the
skin gathered in sharp folds; the brow high-
arched and shaggy; the eye-ball magnificently
large; the curve of the lips just veiled by the
light moustache at the side; the beard short,
double, and short-pointed : all noble and quiet ;
the white sepulchral dust marking like light the
stern angles of the cheek and brow.

This tomb was sculptured in 1424, and is thus
described by one of the most intelligent of the
recent writers who represent the popular feeling
respecting Venetian art :—

"Of the Italian school is also the rich but ugly (ricco
ma non bel) sarcophagus in which repose the ashes of
Tomao Mocenisgo. It may be called one of the last links
which connect the declining art of the Middle Ages with

that of the Renaissance, which was in its rise. We will
not stay to particularise the defects of each of the seven
figures of the front and sides, which represent the cardinal
and theological virtues ; nor will we make any remarks
upon those which stand in the niches above the pavilion,
because we consider them unworthy both of the age and,
reputation of the Florentine school, which was then with
reason considered the most notable in Italy." *

It is well, indeed, not to pause over these defects ;
but it might have been better to have paused a
moment beside that noble image of a king's
mortality.

§ XLI. In the choir of the same Church, St.
Giov. and Paolo, is another tomb, that of the
Dogè Andrea Vendramin. This doge died in
1478, after a short reign of two years, the most
disastrous in the annals of Venice. He died of a
pestilence, which followed the ravage of the Turks,
carried to the shores of the lagoons. He died,
leaving Venice disgraced by sea and land, with
the smoke of hostile devastations rising in the
blue distances of Friuli ; and there was raised
to him the most costly tomb ever bestowed on
her monarchs.

§ XLII. If the writer above quoted was cold
beside the statue of one of the fathers of his
country, he atones for it by his eloquence beside
the tomb of the Vendramin. I must not spoil the
force of Italian superlative by translation.

* Selvatico, "Architettura di Venezia," p. 147.

"Quando si guarda a quella corretta eleganza di profili e di proporzioni, a quella squisitezza d' ornamenti, a quel certo sapore antico che senza ombra d' imitazione traspare da tutta l'opera "—&c. " Sopra ornatissimo zoccolo fornito di squisiti intagli s' alza uno stylobate "—&c. " Sotto le celonne, il predetto stilobate si muta leggiadramente in piedistallo, poi con bella novità di pensiero e di effetto va coronato da un fregio il più gentile che veder si possa "—&c. " Non puossi lasciar senza un cenno l' *arca dove* sta chiuso il doge ; capo lavoro di pensiero e di esecuzione," &c.

There are two pages and a half of closely printed praise, of which the above specimens may suffice; but there is not a word of the statue of the dead from beginning to end. I am myself in the habit of considering this rather an important part of a tomb, and I was especially interested in it here, because Salvatico only echoes the praise of thousands. It is unanimously declared the chief d'œuvre of Renaissance sepulchral work, and pronounced by Cicognara, (also quoted by Selvatico).

"Il vertice a cui l' arti Veneziane si spinsero col ministero del scalpello,"—"The very culminating point to which the Venetian arts attained by ministry of the chisel."

To this culminating point, therefore, covered with dust and cobwebs, I attained, as I did to every tomb of importance in Venice, by the ministry of such ancient ladders as were to be

found in the sacristan's keeping. I was struck
at first by the excessive awkwardness and want
of feeling in the fall of the hand towards the
spectator, for it is thrown off the middle of the
body in order to show its fine cutting. Now the
Mocenigo hand, severe and even stiff in its
articulations, has its veins finely drawn, its
sculptor having justly felt that the delicacy of
the veining expresses alike dignity and age and
birth. The Vendramin hand is far more laboriously cut, but its blunt and clumsy contour at
once makes us feel that all the care has been
thrown away, and well it may be, for it has been
entirely bestowed in cutting gouty wrinkles about
the joints. Such as the hand is, I looked for its
fellow. At first I thought it had been broken off,
but on clearing away the dust, I saw the wretched
effigy had only *one* hand, and was a mere block
on the inner side. The face, heavy and disagree-
able' in its features, is made monstrous by its
semi-sculpture. One side of the forehead is
wrinkled elaborately, the other left smooth; one
side only of the doge's cap is chased; one cheek
only is finished, and the other blocked out and
distorted besides; finally, the ermine robe, which
is elaborately imitated to its utmost lock of hair
and of ground hair on the one side, is blocked
out only on the other: it having been supposed
throughout the work that the effigy was only to
be seen from below, and from one side.

§ XLIII. It was indeed to be so seen by nearly every one; and I do not blame—I should, on the contrary, have praised—the sculpture for regu- lating his treatment of it by its position, if that treatment had not involved, first dishonesty in giving only half a face, a monstrous mask, when we demand true portraiture of the dead; and, secondly, such utter coldness of feeling, as could only consist with an extreme of intellectual and moral degradation: Who, with a heart in his breast, could have stayed his hand as he drew the dim lines of the old man's countenance—unma- jestic once, indeed, but at least, sanctified by the solemnities of death—could have stayed his hand, as he reached the bend of the grey forehead, and measured out the last veins of it at so much the zecchin?

I do not think the reader, if he has feeling, will expect that much talent should be shown in the rest of his work, by the sculptor of this base and senseless lie. The whole monument is one weari- some aggregation of that species of ornamental flourish, which, when it is done with a pen, is called penmanship, and when done with a chisel, should be called chiselmanship; the subject of it being chiefly fat-limbed boys sprawling on dolphins—dolphins incapable of swimming, and dragged along the sea by expanded pocket- handkerchiefs.

But now, reader, comes the very gist and point

of the whole matter. This lying monument to a
dishonoured doge, this culminating pride of the
Renaissance art of Venice, is at least veracious if
in nothing else, in its testimony to the character
of its sculptor. *He was banished from Venice
for forgery* in 1487.*

§ XLIV. I have more to say about this con-
vict's work hereafter; but I pass, at present, to
the second, slighter, but yet more interesting
piece of evidence, which I promised.

The Ducal Palace has two principal façades ;
one towards the sea, the other towards the
Piazzetta. The seaward side, and, as far as its
seventh main arch inclusive, the Piazzetta side,
is work of the early part of the fourteenth century, some of it perhaps even earlier; while the
rest of the Piazzetta side is of the fifteenth. The
difference in age has been gravely disputed by
the Venetian antiquaries, who have examined
many documents on the subject and quoted
some which they never examined. I have myself collated most of the written documents, and
one document more, to which the Venetian antiquaries never thought of referring,—the masonry
of the palace itself.

§ XLV. That masonry changes at the centre of
the eighth arch from the sea angle on the Piazzetta side. It has been of comparatively small

* Selvatico, p. 221.

stones up to that point ; the fifteenth century
work instantly begins with larger stones, " brought
from Istria, a hundred miles away." *   The ninth
shafts from the sea in the lower arcade, and the
seventeenth, which is above it, in the upper
arcade, commence the series of fifteenth century
shaft. These two are somewhat thicker than
the others, and carry the party-wall of the Sala
del Scrutinio. Now, observe, reader. The face
of the palace, from this point to the Porta della
Carta, was built at the instance of that noble
Doge Mocenigo beside whose tomb you have
been standing ; at his instance, and in the beginning of the reign of his successor, Foscari ; that
is to say, circa 1424. This is not disputed ; it is
only disputed that the sea façade is earlier : of
which, however, the proofs are as simple as they
are incontrovertible : for not only the masonry,
but the sculpture, changes at the ninth lower
shaft, and that in the capitals of the shafts both
of the upper and lower arcade : the costumes of
the figures introduced in the sea façade being
purely Giottesque, correspondent with those of
Giotto's work in the Arena Chapel at Padua,
while the costume on the other capitals is
Renaissance-Classic ; and the lions' heads between the arches change at the same point. And
there are a multitude of other evidences in the

* The older work is of Istrian stone also, but of different
quality.

statues of the angles, with which I shall not at present trouble the reader.

§ XLVI. Now, the architect who built under Foscari, in 1424 (remember my date for the decline of Venice, 1418), was obliged to follow the principal forms of the older palace. But he had not the wit to invent new capitals in the same style ; he therefore clumsily copied the old ones. The palace has seventeen main arches on the sea façade, eighteen on the Piazzetta side, which in all are of course carried by thirty-six pillars ; and these pillars I shall always number from right to left, from the angle of the palace at the Ponte della Paglia to that next the Porta della Carta. I number them in this succession, because I thus have the earliest shafts first numbered. So counted, the 1st, the 18th, and the 36th, are the great supports of the angles of the palace ; and the first of the fifteenth century series, being, as above stated, the 9th from the sea on the Piazzetta side, is the 26th of the entire series, and will always in future be so numbered, so that all numbers above twenty-six indicate fifteenth century work, and all below it, fourteenth century, with some exceptional cases of restoration.

Then the copied capitals are : the 28th, copied from the 7th ; the 29th, from the 9th ; the 30th, from the 10th ; the 31st, from the 8th ; the 33rd, from the 12th ; and the 34th, from the 11th ; the

others being dull inventions of the fifteenth
century, except the 36th, which is very nobly,
designed.

§ XLVII. The capitals thus selected from the
earlier portion of the palace for imitation, together with the rest, will be accurately described
hereafter; the point I have here to notice is in
the copy of the ninth capital, which was decorated
(being like the rest, octagonal) with figures of
the eight virtues—Faith, Hope, Charity, Justice,
Temperance, Prudence, Humility (the Venetian
antiquaries call it Humanity!), and Fortitude.
The Virtues of the fourteenth century are somewhat hard-featured; with vivid and living expression, and plain every-day clothes of the time;
Charity has her lap full of apples (perhaps
loaves), and is giving one to a little child, who
stretches his arm for it across a gap in the leafage
of the capital. Fortitude tears open a lion's
jaws; Faith lays her hand on her breast, as she
beholds the Cross; and Hope is praying, while
above her a hand is seen emerging from sunbeams
—the hand of God (according to that of Revelation, "The Lord God giveth them light"); and
the inscription above is "Spes optima in Deo."

§ XLVIII. This design, then, is, rudely and
with imperfect chiselling, imitated by the fifteenth century workmen; the Virtues have lost
their hard features and living expression; they
have now all got Roman noses, and have had

their hair curled. Their actions and emblems are however preserved until we come to Hope: she is still praying, but she is praying to the sun only; *The hand of God is gone.*

Is not this a curious and striking type of the spirit which had then become dominant in the world, forgetting to see God's hand in the light He gave; so that in the issue, when that light opened into the Reformation on the one side, and into full knowledge of ancient literature on the other, the one was arrested and the other perverted.

§ XLIX. Such is the nature of the accidental evidence on which I shall depend for the proof of the inferiority of character in the Renaissance workmen. But the proof of the inferiority of the work itself is not so easy, for in this I have to appeal to judgments which the Renaissance work has itself distorted. I felt this difficulty very forcibly as I read a slight review of my former work, 'The Seven Lamps,' in 'The Architect:' the writer noticed my constant praise of St. Mark's: "Mr. Ruskin thinks it a very beautiful building! We," said 'The Architect,' "think it a very ugly building." I was not surprised at the difference of opinion, but at the thing being considered so completely a subject of opinion. My opponents in matters of painting always assume that there *is* such a thing as a law of right, and that I do not understand it;

but my architectural adversaries appeal to no
law, they simply set their opinion against mine;
and indeed there is no law at present to which
either they or I can appeal. No man can speak
with rational decision of the merits or demerits
of buildings : he may with obstinacy; he may
with resolved adherence to previous prejudices;
but never as if the matter could be otherwise
decided than by majority of votes, or pertinacity
of partizanship. I had always, however, a clear
conviction that there *was* a law in this matter:
that good architecture might be indisputably
discerned and divided from the bad: that the
opposition in their very nature and essence was
clearly visible; and that we were all of us just
as unwise in disputing about the matter without reference to principle, as we should be for de-
bating about the genuineness of a coin without
ringing it. I felt also assured that this law must
be universal if it were conclusive: that it must
enable us to reject all foolish and base work,
and to accept all noble and wise work, without
reference to style or national feeling; that it
must sanction the design of all truly great
nations and times, Gothic or Greek or Arab;
that it must cast off and reprobate the design of
all foolish nations and times, Chinese or Mexican
or Modern European ; and that it must be easily
applicable to all possible architectural inventions
of human mind. I set myself, therefore, to

establish such a law, in full belief that men are
intended, without excessive difficulty, and by
use of their general common sense, to know good
things from bad; and that it is only because they
will not be at the pains required for the discern-
ment, that the world is so widely encumbered
with forgeries and basenesses. I found the work
simpler than I had hoped; the reasonable things
ranged themselves in the order I required, and
the foolish things fell aside, and took themselves
away, so soon as they were looked in the face.
I had then, with respect to Venetian architecture, the choice, either to establish each
division of law in a separate form, as I came
to the features with which it was concerned,
or else to ask the reader's patience, while I
followed out the general inquiry first, and determined with him a code of right and wrong,
to which we might together make retrospective
appeal. I thought this the best, though perhaps
the dullest way; and in these first following
pages I have therefore endeavoured to arrange
those foundations of criticism, on which I shall
rest in my account of Venetian architecture, in a
form clear and simple enough to be intelligible
even to those who never thought of architecture
before. To those who have, much of what is
stated in them will be well-known or self-
evident; but they must not be indignant at a
simplicity on which the whole argument depends

for its usefulness.   From that which appears a
mere truism when first stated, they will find
very singular consequences sometimes following,
—consequences altogether unexpected, and of
considerable importance ; I will not pause here
to dwell on their importance, nor on that of the
thing itself to be done ; for I believe most readers
will at once admit the value of a criterion of
right and wrong in so practical and costly an
art as architecture, and will be apt rather to
doubt the possibility of its attainment than dispute its usefulness if attained.   I invite them,
therefore, to a fair trial, being certain that even
if I should fail in my main purpose, and be
unable to induce in my reader the confidence of
judgment I desire, I shall at least receive his
thanks for the suggestion of consistent reasons,
which may determine hesitating choice, or justify
involuntary preference.   And if I should succeed,
as I hope, in making the Stones of Venice touch-
stones, and detecting, by the mouldering of her
marble, poison more subtle than ever was betrayed by the rending of her crystal ; and if thus
I am enabled to show the baseness of the schools
of architecture and nearly every other art, which
have for three centuries been predominant in
Europe, I believe the result of the inquiry may
be serviceable for proof of a more vital truth
than any at which I have hitherto hinted.   For
observe ; I said the Protestant had despised the

arts, and the Rationalist corrupted them. But
what has the Romanist done meanwhile? He
boasts that it was the papacy which raised the
arts; why could it not support them when it
was left to its own strength? How came it to
yield to the Classicalism which was based on
infidelity, and to oppose no barrier to innova-
tions which have reduced the once faithfully
conceived imagery of its worship to stage decoration? * Shall we not rather find that Romanism,
instead of being a promoter of the arts, has never
shown itself capable of a single great conception
since the separation of Protestantism from its
side?[1] So long as, corrupt though it might be,
no clear witness had been borne against it, so
that it still included in its ranks a vast number
of faithful Christians, so long its arts were noble.
But the witness was borne—the error made
apparent; and Rome, refusing to hear the testimony or forsake the falsehood, has been struck

* Appendix 12 (old edition) : " Romanist Modern Art."

[1] [Perfectly true : but the whole vital value of the truth
was lost by my sectarian ignorance. Protestantism, (so far as
it was still Christianity, and did not consist merely in main-
taining one's own opinion for gospel,) could not separate itself
from the Catholic Church. The so-called Catholics became
themselves sectarians and heretics in casting them out; and
Europe was turned into a mere cockpit, of the theft and fury
of unchristian men of both parties; while, innocent and silent
on the hills and fields, God's people in neglected peace,
everywhere and for ever Catholics, lived and died.]

from that instant with an intellectual palsy, which has not only incapacitated her from any further use of the arts which once were her ministers, but has made her worship the shame of its own shrines, and her worshippers their destroyers.

Come, then, if truths such as these are worth our thoughts ; come, and let us know, before we enter the streets of the Sea city, whether we are indeed to submit ourselves to their undistinguished enchantment, and to look upon the last changes which were wrought on the lifted forms of her palaces, as we should on the capricious towering of summer clouds in the sunset, ere they sank into the deep of night ; or whether, rather, we shall not behold in the brightness of their accumulated marble, pages on which the sentence of her luxury was to be written until the waves should efface it, as they fulfilled— "God has numbered thy kingdom, and finished it."

CHAPTER II.

[FIRST OF SECOND VOLUME IN OLD EDITION.]

THE THRONE.

§ I. IN the olden days of travelling, now to return no more,[a] in which distance could not be vanquished without toil, but in which that toil was rewarded, partly by the power of deliberate survey of the countries through which the journey lay, and partly by the happiness of the evening hours, when, from the top of the last hill he had surmounted, the traveller beheld the quiet village where he was to rest scattered among the meadows beside its valley stream; or, from the long-hoped-for turn in the dusty perspective of the causeway, saw, for the first time, the towers of some famed city, faint in the rays of sunset;—hours of peaceful and thoughtful pleasure, for which the rush of the arrival in the railway station is perhaps not always, or to all men, an equivalent,—in those

[a] [I have as little doubt of their return now, as I had then hope of it, though before that day, I shall have travelled whence there is no return.]

days, I say, when there was something more
to be anticipated and remembered in the first
aspect of each successive halting-place, than a
new arrangement of glass roofing and iron
girder, there were few moments of which the
recollection was more fondly cherished by the
traveller, than that which, as I endeavoured to
describe in the close of the last chapter, brought
him within sight of Venice, as his gondola shot
into the open lagoon from the canal of Mestre.
Not but that the aspect of the city itself was
generally the source of some slight disappoint-
ment, for, seen in this direction, its buildings are
far less characteristic than those of the other
great towns of Italy; but this inferiority was
partly disguised by distance, and more than
atoned for by the strange rising of its walls and
towers out of the midst, as it seemed, of the
deep sea; for it was impossible that the mind or
the eye could at once comprehend the shallow-
ness of the vast sheet of water which stretched
away in leagues of rippling lustre to the north
and south,—or trace the narrow line of islets
bounding it to the east. The salt breeze, the
white, moaning sea-birds, the masses of black
weed separating and disappearing gradually, in
knots of heaving shoal, under the advance of the
steady tide, all proclaimed it to be indeed the
ocean on whose bosom the great city rested so
calmly; not such blue, soft, lake-like ocean as

bathes the Neapolitan promontories, or sleeps
beneath the marble rocks of Genoa, but a sea
with the bleak power of our own northern
waves, yet subdued into a strange, spacious
rest, and changed from its angry pallor into a
field of burnished gold, as the sun declined
behind the belfry tower of the lonely island
church, fitly named "St. George of the Seaweed."
As the boat drew nearer to the city, the coast
which the traveller had just left sank behind
him into one long, low, sad-coloured[b] line, tufted
irregularly with brushwood and willows: but,
at what seemed its northern extremity, the hills
of Argua rose in a dark cluster of purple
pyramids, balanced on the bright mirage of the
lagoon; two or three smooth surges of inferior
hill extended themselves about their roots, and
beyond these, beginning with the craggy peaks
above Vicenza, the chain of the Alps girded the
whole horizon to the north—a wall of jagged
blue, here and there showing through its clefts
a wilderness of misty precipices, fading far back
into the recesses of Cadore, and itself rising and
breaking away eastward, where the sun struck
opposite upon its snow, into mighty fragments
of peaked light, standing up behind the barred
clouds of evening, one after another, countless,
the crown of the Adrian Sea, until the eye

[b] [Nonsense. I might as truly have said 'merry-coloured.'
It is simply of the colour of any other distant country.]

turned back from pursuing them, to rest upon
the nearer burning of the campaniles of Murano,
and on the great city, where it magnified itself
along the waves, as the quick, silent pacing of
the gondola drew nearer and nearer.[c] And at
last, when its walls were reached, and the out-
most of its untrodden streets were entered, not
through towered gate or guarded rampart, but
as a deep inlet between two rocks of coral in
the Indian sea; when first upon the traveller's
sight opened the long ranges of columned
palaces,—each with its black boat moored at the
portal,—each with its image cast down, beneath
its feet, upon that green pavement which every
breeze broke into new fantasies of rich tessel-
lation ;—when first, at the extremity of the
bright vista, the shadowy Rialto threw its
colossal curve slowly forth from behind the
palace of the Camerlenghi; that strange curve,
so delicate, so adamantine, strong as a mountain
cavern, graceful as a bow just bent ;—when first
before its moonlike circumference was all risen,
the gondolier's cry, "Ah! Stalì,"[*] struck sharp
upon the ear, and the prow turned aside under

[c] [All this is quite right. The group of precipices above the
centre of the Alpine line is the finest I know in any view of
the chain from the south, and the extent of white peaks to
the north-east always takes me by renewed surprise, in clear
evenings.]

[*] Appendix 1 (old edition) : "The Gondolier's Cry."

the mighty cornices that half met over the narrow canal, where the plash of the water followed close and loud, ringing along the marble by the boat's side; and when at last that boat darted forth upon the breadth of silver sea, across which the front of the Ducal Palace, flushed with its sanguine veins, looks to the snowy dome of Our Lady of Salvation,* it was no marvel that the mind should be so deeply entranced by the visionary charm of a scene so beautiful and so strange, as to forget the darker truths of its history and its being. Well might it seem that such a city had owed her existence rather to the rod of the enchanter than the fear of the fugitive; that the waters which encircled her had been chosen for the mirror of her state, rather than the shelter of her nakedness; and that all which in nature was wild or merciless,—Time and Decay, as well as the waves and tempests,—had been won to adorn her instead of to destroy, and might still spare, for ages to come, that beauty which seemed to have fixed for its throne the sands of the hour-glass as well as of the sea.

§ II. And although the last few eventful years, fraught with change to the face of the whole earth, have been more fatal in their influence on Venice than the five hundred that

---

* Appendix 2 (old edition) : " Our Lady of Salvation."

preceded them; though the noble landscape of
approach to her can now be seen no more, or
seen only by a glance, as the engine slackens its
rushing on the iron line; and though many of
her palaces are for ever defaced, and many in
desecrated ruins, there is still so much of magic
in her aspect, that the hurried traveller, who
must leave her before the wonder of that first
aspect has been worn away, may still be led to
forget the humility of her origin, and to shut
his eyes to the depth of her desolation. They,[d]
at least, are little to be envied, in whose hearts
the great charities of the imagination lie dead,
and for whom the fancy has no power to repress
the importunity of painful impressions, or to
raise what is ignoble, and disguise what is
discordant, in a scene so rich in its remem-
brances, so surpassing in its beauty. But for
this work of the imagination there must be no
permission during the task which is before us.
The impotent feelings of romance, so singularly
characteristic of this century, may indeed gild,
but never save, the remains of those mightier
ages to which they are attached like climbing
flowers; and they must be torn away from the

[d] [This is a true, and, as far as I can judge of my own
writing, one of my best finished passages, to the close of the
paragraph, except that the charity of imagination, in the
beginning of the clause, should have been more directly
connected with the indolence of the imagination at its end.]

magnificent fragments, if we would see them as they stood in their own strength. Those feelings, always as fruitless as they are fond, are in Venice not only incapable of protecting, but even of discerning, the objects to which they ought to have been attached. The Venice of modern fiction and drama is a thing of yesterday, a mere efflorescence of decay, a stage dream which the first ray of daylight must dissipate into dust. No prisoner, whose name is worth remembering, or whose sorrow deserved sympathy, ever crossed that "Bridge of Sighs," which is the centre of the Byronic ideal of Venice; no great merchant of Venice ever saw that Rialto under which the traveller now passes with breathless interest : the statue which Byron makes Faliero address as of one of his great ancestors, was erected to a soldier of fortune a hundred and fifty years after Faliero's death; and the most conspicuous parts of the city have been so entirely altered in the course of the last three centuries, that if Henry Dandolo or Francis Foscari could be summoned from their tombs, and stood each on the deck of his galley at the entrance of the Grand Canal, —that renowned entrance, the painter's favourite subject, the novelist's favourite scene, where the water first narrows by the steps of the Church of La Salute°—the mighty Doges would not

° [Little thought I that, five-and-twenty years after writing

know in what spot of the world they stood,
would literally not recognise one stone of the
great city, for whose sake, and by whose
ingratitude, their gray hairs had been brought
down with bitterness to the grave. The remains
of *their* Venice lie hidden behind the cumbrous
masses which were the delight of the nation in
its dotage; hidden in many a grass-grown court,
and silent pathway, and lightless canal, where
the slow waves have sapped their foundations
for five hundred years, and must soon prevail
over them for ever. It must be our task to
glean and gather them forth, and restore out of
them some faint image of the lost city; more
gorgeous a thousandfold than that which now
exists, yet not created in the day-dream of the
prince, nor by the ostentation of the noble, but
built by iron hands and patient hearts, contending against the adversity of nature and the
fury of man: so that its wonderfulness cannot
be grasped by the indolence of imagination, but
only after frank inquiry into the true nature of
that wild and solitary scene, whose restless tides
and trembling sands did indeed shelter the birth
of the city, but long denied her dominion.

§ III. When the eye falls casually on a map of
Europe, there is no feature by which it is more

this sentence, I should revise it again for press with this piece
of the canal lapping under my window (Casa Ferro, 21st
December, 1876).]

likely to be arrested than the strange sweeping loop formed by the junction of the Alps and Apennines, and enclosing the great basin of Lombardy. This return of the mountain chain upon itself causes a vast difference in the character of the distribution of its débris on its opposite sides. The rock fragments and sediments which the torrents on the north side of the Alps bear into the plains are distributed over a vast extent of country, and, though here and there lodged in beds of enormous thickness, soon permit the firm substrata to appear from underneath them; but all the torrents which descend from the southern side of the High Alps, and from the northern slope of the Apennines, meet concentrically in the recess or mountain bay which the two ridges enclose; every fragment which thunder breaks out of their battlements, and every grain of dust which the summer rain washes from their pastures, is at last laid at rest in the blue sweep of the Lombardic plain; and that plain must have risen within its rocky barriers as a cup fills with wine, but for two contrary influences which continually depress, or disperse from its surface, the accumulation of the ruins of ages.

§ IV. I will not tax the reader's faith in modern science' by insisting on the singular depression of

[I wish I could now appeal to his faith in anything else !]

the surface of Lombardy, which appears for many
centuries to have taken place steadily and continually; the main fact with which we have to
do is the gradual transport, by the Po, and its
great collateral rivers, of vast masses of the finer
sediment to the sea. The character of the
Lombardic plain is most strikingly expressed
by the ancient walls of its cities, composed for
the most part of large rounded Alpine pebbles
alternating with narrow courses of brick; and
was curiously illustrated in 1848, by the ram-
parts of these same pebbles thrown up four or
five feet high round every field, to check the
Austrian cavalry in the battle under the walls
of Verona. The finer dust among which these
pebbles are dispersed is taken up by the rivers,
fed into continual strength by the Alpine snow,
so that, however pure their waters may be when
they issue from the lakes at the foot of the great
chain, they become of the colour and opacity of
clay before they reach the Adriatic; the sediment
which they bear is at once thrown down as they
enter the sea, forming a vast belt of low land
along the eastern coast of Italy. The powerful
stream of the Po of course builds forward the
fastest; on each side of it, north and south, there
is a tract of marsh, fed by more feeble streams,
and less liable to rapid change than the delta of
the central river. In one of these tracts is built
RAVENNA, and in the other, VENICE.

§ v. What circumstances directed the peculiar arrangement of this great belt of sediment in the earliest times, it is not here the place to inquire. It is enough for us to know that from the mouths of the Adige to those of the Piave, there stretches, at a variable distance of from three to five miles from the actual shore, a bank of sand, divided into long islands by narrow channels of sea. The space between this bank and the true shore consists of the sedimentary deposits from these and other rivers, a great plain of calcareous mud, covered, in the neighbourhood of Venice, by the sea at high water, to the depth in most places of a foot or a foot and a half, and nearly everywhere exposed at low tide, but divided by an intricate network of narrow and winding channels, from which the sea never retires. In some places, according to the run of the currents, the land has risen into marshy islets, consolidated, some by art, and some by time, into ground firm enough to be built upon, or fruitful enough to be cultivated: in others, on the contrary, it has not reached the sea level; so that, at the average low water, shallow lakelets glitter among its irregularly exposed fields of seaweed. In the midst of the largest of these, increased in importance by the confluence of several large river channels towards one of the openings in the sea bank, the city of Venice itself is built, on a crowded cluster of islands; the various plots of higher ground

which appear to the north and south of this
central cluster, have at different periods been
also thickly inhabited, and now bear, according
to their size, the remains of cities, villages, or
isolated convents and churches, scattered among
spaces of open ground, partly waste and encumbered by ruins, partly under cultivation for
the supply of the metropolis.

§ VI. The average rise and fall of the tide is
about three feet (varying considerably with the
seasons*) ; but this fall, on so flat a shore, is
enough to cause continual movement in the
waters, and in the main canals to produce a
reflux which frequently runs like a mill stream.
At high water no land is visible for many miles
to the north or south of Venice, except in the
form of small islands crowned with towers or
gleaming with villages : there is a channel, some
three miles wide, between the city and the mainland, and some mile and a half wide between it
and the sandy breakwater called the Lido, which
divides the lagoon from the Adriatic, but which
is so low as hardly to disturb the impression of
the city's having been built in the midst of the
ocean, although the secret of its true position is
partly, yet not painfully, betrayed by the clusters
of piles set to mark the deep-water channels,
which undulate far away in spotty chains like

---

* Appendix 3 (old edition) : "Tides of Venice."

the studded backs of huge sea-snakes, and by
the quick glittering of the crisped and crowded
waves that flicker and dance before the strong
winds upon the unlifted level of the shallow sea.
But the scene is widely different at low tide. A
fall of eighteen or twenty inches is enough to
show ground over the greater part of the
lagoon; and at the complete ebb the city is
seen standing in the midst of a dark plain of
seaweed, of gloomy green, except only where
the larger branches of the Brenta and its associated streams converge towards the port of
the Lido. Through this salt and sombre plain
the gondola and the fishing-boat advance by
tortuous channels, seldom more than four or
five feet deep, and often so choked with slime
that the heavier keels furrow the bottom till
their crossing tracks are seen through the clear
sea water like the ruts upon a wintry road, and
the oar leaves blue gashes upon the ground at
every stroke, or is entangled among the thick
weed that fringes the banks with the weight of
its sullen waves, leaning to and fro upon the
uncertain sway of the exhausted tide. The
scene is often profoundly oppressive, even at
this day, when every plot of higher ground
bears some fragment of fair building: but, in
order to know what it was once, let the traveller
follow in his boat at evening the windings of
some unfrequented channel far into the midst

of the melancholy plain; let him remove, in
his imagination, the brightness of the great city
that still extends itself in the distance, and the
walls and towers from the islands that are near;
and so wait, until the bright investiture and sweet
warmth of the sunset are withdrawn from the
waters, and the black desert of their shore lies
in its nakedness beneath the night, pathless,
comfortless, infirm, lost in dark languor and
fearful silence, except where the salt runlets
plash into the tideless pools, or the sea-birds
flit from their margins with a questioning cry;
and he will be enabled to enter in some sort
into the horror of heart with which this solitude
was anciently chosen by man for his habitation.
They little thought, who first drove the stakes
into the sand, and strewed the ocean reeds for
their rest, that their children were to be the
princes of that ocean, and their palaces its pride;
and yet, in the great natural laws that rule that
sorrowful wilderness, let it be remembered what
strange preparation had been made for the things
which no human imagination could have foretold,
and how the whole existence and fortune of the
Venetian nation were anticipated or compelled,
by the setting of those bars and doors to the
rivers and the sea. Had deeper currents divided
their islands, hostile navies would again and again
have reduced the rising city into servitude; had
stronger surges beaten their shores, all the richness

and refinement of the Venetian architecture must have been exchanged for the walls and bulwarks of an ordinary seaport. Had there been no tide, as in other parts of the Mediterranean, the narrow canals of the city would have become noisome, and the marsh in which it was built pestiferous. Had the tide only been a foot or eighteen inches higher in its rise, the water-access to the doors of the palaces would have been impossible; even as it is, there is sometimes a little difficulty, at the ebb, in landing without setting foot upon the lower and slippery steps; and the highest tides sometimes enter the courtyards, and overflow the entrance halls. Eighteen inches more of difference between the level of the flood and ebb would have rendered the doorsteps of every palace, at low water, a treacherous mass of weeds and limpets, and the entire system of water-carriage for the higher classes, in their easy and daily intercourse, must have been done away with. The streets of the city would have been widened, its network of canals filled up, and all the peculiar character of the place and the people destroyed.

§ VII. The reader may perhaps have felt some pain in the contrast between this faithful view of the site of the Venetian Throne, and the romantic conception of it which we ordinarily form; but this pain, if he have felt it, ought to be more than counterbalanced by the value of the instance thus afforded to us at once of the inscrutableness and the wisdom of the ways of God. If, two thousand years ago, we had been permitted to watch the slow settling of the slime of those turbid rivers into the polluted sea, and the gaining upon its deep and fresh waters of the lifeless, impassable, unvoyageable plain, how little could we have understood the purpose with which those islands were shaped out of the void, and the torpid waters enclosed with their desolate walls of sand! How little could we have known, any more than of what now seems to us most distressful, dark, and objectless, the glorious aim which was then in the mind of Him in whose hands are all the corners of the earth! how little imagined that in the laws which were stretching forth the gloomy margins of those fruitless banks, and feeding the bitter grass among their shallows, there was indeed a preparation, and *the only preparation possible,* for the founding of a city which was to be set like a golden clasp on the girdle of the earth ;— to write her history on the white scrolls of the sea-surges, and to word it in their thunder,— and to gather and give forth, in world-wide pulsation, the glory of the West and of the East, from the burning heart of her Fortitude and Splendour !

CHAPTER III.

[SECOND OF SECOND VOLUME IN THE OLD EDITION.]

TORCELLO.

§ I. SEVEN miles to the north of Venice, the banks of sand, which near the city rise little above low-water mark, attain by degrees a higher level, and knit themselves at last into fields of salt morass, raised here and there into shapeless mounds, and intercepted by narrow creeks of sea. One of the feeblest of these inlets, after winding for some time among buried fragments of masonry, and knots of sunburnt weeds whitened with webs of fucus, stays itself in an utterly stagnant pool beside a plot of greener grass covered with ground ivy and violets. On this mound is built a rude brick campanile, of the commonest Lombardic type, which if we ascend towards evening (and there are none to hinder us, the door of its ruinous staircase, swinging idly on its hinges), we may command from it one of the most notable scenes in this wide world of ours.

Far as the eye can reach, a waste of wild sea

moor, of a lurid ashen grey; not like our northern
moors, with their jet-black pools and purple
heath, but lifeless, the colour of sackcloth with
the corrupted sea-water soaking through the
roots of its arid weeds, and gleaming hither and
thither through its snaky channels. No gathering of fantastic mists, no coursing of clouds
across it; but melancholy clearness of space in
the warm sunset, oppressive, reaching to the
horizon of its level gloom. To the very horizon,
on the north-east; but to the north and west,
there is a blue line of higher land along the
border of it, and above this, but farther back, a
misty band of mountains, touched with snow.
To the east, the paleness and roar of the Adriatic,
louder at momentary intervals as the surf breaks
on the bars of sand; to the south, the widening
branches of the calm lagoon, alternately purple
and pale green, as they reflect the evening clouds
or twilight sky; and almost beneath our feet, on
the same field which sustains the tower we gaze
from, a group of four buildings, two of them little
larger than cottages (though built of stone, and
one adorned by a quaint belfry), the third an octagonal chapel, of which we can see but little more
than the flat red roof with its rayed tiling, the
fourth a considerable church with nave and aisles,
but of which, in like manner, we can see little but
the long central ridge and lateral slopes of roof,
which the sunlight separates in one glowing mass

from the green field beneath and grey moor beyond. There are no living creatures near the buildings, nor any vestige of village or city round about them. They lie like a little company of ships becalmed on a far-away sea.

§ II. Then look farther to the south. Beyond the widening branches of the lagoon, and rising out of the bright lake into which they gather, there are a multitude of towers, dark and scattered among square-set shapes of clustered palaces, a long and irregular line fretting the southern sky.

Mother and daughter,—you behold them, both in their widowhood,—TORCELLO, and VENICE.

Thirteen hundred years ago, the grey moorland looked as it does this day, and the purple mountains stood as radiantly in the deep distances of evening; but on the line of the horizon, there were strange fires mixed with the light of sunset, and the lament of many human voices mixed with the fretting of the waves on their ridges of sand. The flames rose from the ruins of Altinum; the lament from the multitude of its people, seeking, like Israel of old, a refuge from the sword in the paths of the sea.

The cattle are feeding and resting upon the site of the city that they left; the mower's scythe swept this day at dawn over the chief street of the city that they built; and the swathes of soft grass are now sending up their scent into

the night air, the only incense that fills the
temple of their ancient worship. Let us go
down into that little space of meadow land.

§ III. The inlet which runs nearest to the
base of the campanile is not that by which Torcello is commonly approached. Another, somewhat broader, and overhung by alder copse, winds
out of the lagoon up to the very edge of the little
meadow which was once the Piazza of the city,
and there, stayed by a few grey stones which
present some semblance of a quay, forms its
boundary at one extremity. Hardly larger than
an ordinary English farmyard, and roughly enclosed on each side by broken palings and hedges
of honeysuckle and briar, the narrow field retires
from the water's edge, traversed by a scarcely
traceable footpath, for some forty or fifty paces,
and then expanding into the form of a small
square, with buildings on three sides of it, the
fourth being that which opens to the water.
Two of these, that on our left and that in front
of us as we approach from the canal, are so small
that they might well be taken for the outhouses
of the farm, though the first is a conventual
building, and the other aspires to the title of the
" Palazzo publico," both dating as far back as the
beginning of the fourteenth century; the third,
the octagonal church of Santo Fosca, is far more
ancient than either, yet hardly on a larger scale.
Though the pillars of the portico which surrounds

it are of pure Greek marble, and their capitals
are enriched with delicate sculpture, they, and
the arches they sustain, together only raise the
roof to the height of a cattle-shed ; and the first
strong impression which the spectator receives
from the whole scene is, that whatever sin it may
have been which has on this spot been visited
with so utter a desolation, it could not at least
have been ambition. Nor will this impression be
diminished as we approach, or enter, the larger
church, to which the whole group of building is
subordinate. It has evidently been built by men
in flight and distress,[a] who sought in the hurried
erection of their island church such a shelter for
their earnest and sorrowful worship as, on the
one hand, could not attract the eyes of their
enemies by its splendour, and yet, on the other,
might not awaken too bitter feelings by its contrast with the churches which they had seen destroyed. There is visible everywhere a simple and
tender effort to recover some of the form of the
temples which they had loved, and to do honour
to God by that which they were erecting, while
distress and humiliation prevented the desire, and
prudence precluded the admission, either of luxury

---

[a] [A great deal of this talk is flighty, and some of it, fallacious ; I should have to rewrite it all, or must leave it alone.
Aquileia, not Torcello, was the true mother of Venice ; but the
sentiment and essential truth of general principle in the chapter
induce me to reprint the available part of it in this edition.]

of ornament or magnificence of plan. The exterior
is absolutely devoid of decoration, with the exception only of the western entrance and the
lateral door, of which the former has carved side-
posts and architrave, and the latter, crosses of
rich sculpture ; while the massy stone shutters
of the windows, turning on huge rings of stone,
which answer the double purpose of stanchions
and brackets, cause the whole building rather to
resemble a refuge from Alpine storm than the
cathedral of a populous city ; and, internally, the
two solemn mosaics of the eastern and western
extremities,—one representing the Last Judgment, the other the Madonna, her tears falling
as her hands are raised to bless,—and the noble
range of pillars which enclose the space between,
terminated by the high throne for the pastor
and the semicircular raised seats for the superior
clergy, are expressive at once of the deep sorrow
and the sacred courage of men who had no home
left them upon earth, but who looked for one to
come, of men " persecuted but not forsaken, cast
down but not destroyed." *

*   *   *   *   *

§ IX. And observe this choice of subjects. It
is indeed possible that the walls of the nave and
aisles, which are now whitewashed, may have
been covered with fresco or mosaic, and thus have

* Five paragraphs (IV.-VIII.) of the old edition are here
omitted.

supplied a. series of subjects, on the choice of
which we cannot speculate. I do not, however,
find record of the destruction of any such works;
and I am rather inclined to believe that at any
rate the central division of the building was
originally decorated, as it is now, simply by
mosaics representing Christ, the Virgin, and the
Apostles, at one extremity, and Christ coming
· to judgment at· the other. And if so, I repeat,
observe the significance of this choice. Most
other early churches are covered with imagery
sufficiently suggestive of the vivid interest of the
builders in the history and occupations of the
world. Symbols or representations of political
events, portraits of living persons, and sculptures
of satirical, grotesque, or trivial subjects are of
constant occurrence, mingled with the more strictly
appointed representations of scriptural or ecclesiastical history ; but at Torcello even these usual,
and one should have thought almost necessary,
successions of Bible events do not appear. The
mind of the worshipper was fixed entirely upon
two great facts, to him the most precious of all
facts—the present mercy of Christ to His Church,
and His future coming to judge the world. That
Christ's mercy was, at this period, supposed chiefly
to be attainable through the pleading of the
Virgin, and that therefore beneath the figure of
the Redeemer is seen that of the weeping
Madonna in the act of intercession, may indeed

be matter of sorrow to the Protestant beholder,[b]
but ought not to blind him to the earnestness
and singleness of the faith with which these men
sought their sea-solitudes; not in hope of founding new dynasties, or entering upon new epochs
of prosperity, but only to humble themselves
before God, and to pray that in His infinite
mercy He would hasten the time when the sea
should give up the dead which were in it, and
Death and Hell give up the dead which were in
them, and when they might enter into the better
kingdom, " where the wicked cease from troubling
and the weary are at rest."

§ x. Nor were the strength and elasticity of
their minds, even in the least matters, diminished
by thus looking forward to the close of all things.
On the contrary, nothing is more remarkable
than the finish and beauty of all the portions of
the building, which seem to have been actually
executed for the place they occupy in the present
structure : the rudest are those which they brought
with them from the mainland; the best and most
beautiful, those which appear to have been carved
for their island church: of these, the new
capitals already noticed, and the exquisite panel
ornaments of the chancel screen, are the most
conspicuous; the latter form a low wall across

---

[b] [The Protestant beholder may now advisedly reserve his
sorrow for those of his own sect, now numerous enough, who
deny the efficacy of prayer altogether.]

the church, between the six small shafts whose
places are seen in the plan ; and serve to enclose
a space raised two steps above the level of the
nave, destined for the singers, and indicated also
in the plan by an open line *a b c d*. The bas-
reliefs on this low screen are groups of pea-
cocks and lions, two face to face on each panel,
rich and fantastic beyond description, though not
expressive of very accurate knowledge either of
leonine or pavonine forms. And it is not until
we pass to the back of the stair of the pulpit,
which is connected with the northern extremity
of this screen, that we find evidence of the haste
with which the church was constructed.

§ xi. The pulpit, however, is not among the
least noticeable of its features. It is sustained
on the four small detached shafts marked at *p* in
the plan, between the two pillars at the north side
of the screen ; both pillars and pulpit studiously
plain, while the staircase which ascends to it is a
compact mass of masonry (shaded in the plan),
faced by carved slabs of marble ; the parapet of
the staircase being also formed of solid blocks, like
paving stones, lightened by rich, but not deep,
exterior carving. Now these blocks, or at least
those which adorn the staircase towards the aisle,
have been brought from the mainland ; and,
being of size and shape not easily to be adjusted
to the proportions of the stair, the architect has
cut out of them pieces of the size he needed,

utterly regardless of the subject or symmetry of
the original design. The pulpit is not the only
place where this rough procedure has been permitted ; at the lateral door of the church are two
crosses, cut out of slabs of marble, formerly
covered with rich sculpture over their whole
surfaces, of which portions are left on the surface
of the crosses ; the lines of the original design
being, of course, just as arbitrarily cut by the
incisions between the arms, as the patterns upon
a piece of silk which has been shaped anew.
The fact is, that in all early Romanesque work,
large surfaces are covered with sculpture for the
sake of enrichment only ; sculpture which indeed
had always meaning, because it was easier for the
sculptor to work with some chain of thought to
guide his chisel, than without any ; but it was
not always intended, or at least not always
hoped, that this chain of thought might be
traced by the spectator. All that was proposed
appears to have been the enrichment of surface,
so as to make it delightful to the eye ; and this
being once understood, a decorated piece of marble
became to the architect just what a piece of lace
or embroidery is to a dressmaker, who takes of it
such portions as she may require, with little regard to the places where the patterns are divided.
And though it may appear, at first sight, that the
procedure is indicative of bluntness and rudeness
of feeling, we may perceive, upon reflection, that

it may also indicate the redundance of power which sets little price upon its own exertion. When a barbarous nation builds its fortress-walls out of fragments of the refined architecture it has overthrown, we can read nothing but its savageness in the vestiges of art which may thus chance to have been preserved ; but when the new work is equal, if not superior, in execution, to the pieces of the older art which are associated with it, we may justly conclude that the rough treatment to which the latter have been subjected is rather a sign of the hope of doing better things than of want of feeling for those already accomplished. And, in general, this careless fitting of ornament is, in very truth, an evidence of life in the school of builders, and of their making a due distinction between work which is to be used for architectural effect, and work which is to possess an abstract perfection ; and it commonly shows also that the exertion of design is so easy to them, and their fertility so inexhaustible, that they feel no remorse in using somewhat injuriously what they can replace with so slight an effort.

§ XII. It appears, however, questionable in the present instance, whether, if the marbles had not been carved to his hand, the architect would have taken the trouble to enrich them. For the execution of the rest of the pulpit is studiously simple, and it is in this respect that its design possesses, it seems to me, an interest

to the religious spectator greater than he will
take in any other portion of the building. It is
supported, as I said, on a group of four slender
shafts; itself of a slightly oval form, extending
nearly from one pillar of the nave to the next, so
as to give the preacher free room for the.action of
the entire person, which always gives an unaffected
impressiveness to the eloquence of the southern
nations. In the centre of its curved front, a small
bracket and detached shaft sustain the projection
of a narrow marble desk (occupying the place of
a cushion in a modern pulpit), which is hollowed
out into a shallow curve on the upper surface,
leaving a ledge at the bottom of the slab, so that
a book laid upon it, or rather into it, settles itself
there, opening as if by instinct, but without the
least chance of slipping to the side, or in any
way moving beneath the preacher's hands. Six
balls, or rather almonds, of purple marble veined
with white, are set round the edge of the pulpit,
and form its only decoration. Perfectly graceful, but severe and almost cold in its simplicity,
built for permanence and service, so that no
single member, no stone of it, could be spared,
and yet all are firm and uninjured as when they
were first set together, it stands in venerable
contrast both with the fantastic pulpits of
mediæval cathedrals and with the rich furniture
of those of our modern churches. It is worth
while pausing for a moment to consider how far

the manner of decorating a pulpit may have influence on the efficiency of its service, and whether our modern treatment of this, to us all-important, feature of a church be the best possible.* c

§ XIII. When the sermon is good we need not much concern ourselves about the form of the pulpit. But sermons cannot always be good; and I believe that the temper in which the congregation set themselves to listen may be in some degree modified by their perception of fitness or unfitness, impressiveness or vulgarity, in the disposition of the place appointed for the speaker —not to the same degree, but somewhat in the same way, that they may be influenced by his own gestures or expression, irrespective of the sense of what he says. I believe, therefore, in the first place, that pulpits ought never to be highly decorated; the speaker is apt to look mean or diminutive if the pulpit is either on a very large scale or covered with splendid ornament, and if the interest of the sermon should flag the mind is instantly tempted to wander. I have observed that in almost all cathedrals, when the pulpits are peculiarly magnificent, sermons are not often preached from them; but rather, and especially if for any important purpose, from some temporary erection in other parts of

* Appendix 5 (old edition) : " Modern Pulpits." c [The next two paragraphs, §§ XIII. and XIV., are very good.]

the building; and though this may often be done because the architect has consulted the effect upon the eye more than the convenience of the ear in the placing of his larger pulpit, I think it also proceeds in some measure from a natural dislike in the preacher to match himself with the magnificence of the rostrum, lest the sermon should not be thought worthy of the place. Yet this will rather hold of the colossal sculptures, and pyramids of fantastic tracery which encumber the pulpits of Flemish and German churches, than of the delicate mosaics and ivory-like carving of the Romanesque basilicas, for when the form is kept simple, much loveliness of colour and costliness of work may be introduced, and yet the speaker not be thrown into the shade by them.

§ xiv. But, in the second place, whatever ornaments we admit ought clearly to be of a chaste, grave, and noble kind; and what furniture we employ, evidently more for the honouring of God's word than for the ease of the preacher. For there are two ways of regarding a sermon, either as a human composition, or a Divine message. If we look upon it entirely as the first, and require our clergymen to finish it with their utmost care and learning, for our better delight whether of ear or intellect, we shall necessarily be led to expect much formality and stateliness in its delivery, and to think that all

is not well if the pulpit have not a golden
fringe round it, and a goodly cushion in front of
it, and if the sermon be not fairly written in a
black book, to be smoothed upon the cushion in
a majestic manner before beginning; all this we
shall duly come to expect: but we shall at the
same time consider the treatise thus prepared
as something to which it is our duty to listen
without restlessness for half an hour or three
quarters, but which, when that duty has been
decorously performed, we may dismiss from our
minds in happy confidence of being provided
with another when next it shall be necessary.
But if once we begin to regard the preacher,
whatever his faults, as a man sent with a message
to us, which it is a matter of life or death whether
we hear or refuse; if we look upon him as set in
charge over many spirits in danger of ruin, and
having allowed to him but an hour or two in the
seven days to speak to them; if we make some
endeavour to conceive how precious these hours
ought to be to him, a small vantage on the side
of God after his flock have been exposed for six
days together to the full weight of the world's
temptation, and he has been forced to watch the
thorn and the thistle springing in their hearts,
and to see what wheat had been scattered there
snatched from the wayside by this wild bird and
the other; and at last, when breathless and
weary with the week's labour, they give him this

interval of imperfect and languid hearing, he
has but thirty minutes to get at the separate
hearts of a thousand men, to convince them of all
their weaknesses, to shame them for all their sins,
to warn them of all their dangers, to try by this
way and that to stir the hard fastenings of those
doors where the Master Himself has stood and
knocked,—yet none opened, and to call at the
openings of those dark streets where Wisdom
herself hath stretched forth her hands, and no
man regarded,—thirty minutes to raise the dead
in,—let us but once understand and feel this,
and we shall look with changed eyes upon that
frippery of gay furniture about the place from
which the message of judgment must be delivered,
which either breathes upon the dry bones that
they may live, or, if ineffectual, remains recorded
in condemnation, perhaps against the utterer
and listener alike, but assuredly against one of
them. We shall not so easily bear with the silk
and gold upon the seat of judgment, nor with
ornament of oratory in the mouth of the mes-
senger ; we shall wish that his words may be
simple, even when they are sweetest, and the
place from which he speaks like a marble rock in
the desert, about which the people have gathered
in their thirst.

§ xv. But the severity which is so marked in
the pulpit at Torcello is still more striking in the
raised seats and episcopal throne which occupy

the curve of the apse. The arrangement at first
somewhat recalls to the mind that of the Roman
amphitheatres; the flight of steps which lead up
to the central throne divides the curve of the
continuous steps or seats (it appears in the first
three ranges questionable which were intended,
for they seem too high for the one, and too low
and close for the other), exactly as in an amphi-
theatre the stairs for access intersect the sweeping ranges of seats. But in the very rudeness
of this arrangement, and especially in the want
of all appliances of comfort (for the whole is of
marble, and the arms of the central throne are
not for convenience, but for distinction, and to
separate it more conspicuously from the undivided
seats), there is a dignity which no furniture of
stalls nor carving of canopies ever could attain,
and well worth the contemplation of the Protestant, both as sternly significative of an episcopal
authority which in the early days of the Church
was never disputed, and as dependent for all its
impressiveness on the utter absence of any
expression either of pride or self-indulgence.

§ XVI. But there is one more circumstance
which we ought to remember as giving peculiar
significance to the position which the episcopal
throne occupies in this island church, namely
that in the minds of all early Christians the
Church itself was most frequently symbolised
under the image of a ship, of which the bishop

was the pilot. Consider the force which this
symbol would assume in the imaginations of
men to whom the spiritual Church had become
an ark of refuge in the midst of a destruction
hardly less terrible than that from which the
eight souls were saved of old, a destruction in
which the wrath of man had become as broad
as the earth, and as merciless as the sea, and
who saw the actual and literal edifice of the
Church raised up, itself like an ark in the midst
of the waters. No marvel if, with the surf of the
Adriatic rolling between them and the shores of
their birth, from which they were separated for
ever, they should have looked upon each other
as the disciples did when the storm came down
on the Tiberias Lake, and have yielded ready
and loving obedience to those who ruled them
in His name, who had there rebuked the winds
and commanded stillness to the sea. And if the
stranger would yet learn in what spirit it was
that the dominion of Venice was begun, and in
what strength she went forth conquering and to
conquer, let him not seek to estimate the wealth
of her arsenals, or number of her armies; nor
look upon the pageantry of her palaces, nor
enter into the secrets of her councils; but let
him ascend the highest tier of the stern ledges
that sweep round the altar of Torcello, and then,
looking as the pilot did of old along the marble
ribs of the goodly temple-ship, let him re-people

its veined deck with the shadows of its dead mariners, and strive to feel in himself the strength of heart that was kindled within them, when first, after the pillars of it had settled in the sand, and the roof of it had been closed against the angry sky that was still reddened by the fires of their homesteads,—first, within the shelter of its knitted walls, amidst the murmur of the waste of waves and the beating of the wings of the sea-birds round the rock that was strange to them,—rose that ancient hymn, in the power of their gathered voices:

THE SEA IS HIS AND HE MADE IT :
AND HIS HANDS PREPARED THE DRY LAND.

CHAPTER IV.

[FOURTH OF SECOND VOLUME IN OLD EDITION.]

· ST. MARK'S.

§ I. "AND so Barnabas took Mark, and sailed unto Cyprus." If as the shores of Asia lessened upon his sight, the spirit of prophecy had entered into the heart of the weak disciple who had turned back when his hand was on the plough, and who had been judged, by the chiefest of Christ's captains, unworthy thenceforward to go forth with him to the work,* how wonderful would he have thought it, that by the lion symbol in future ages he was to be represented among men! how woful, that the war-cry of his name should so often reanimate the rage of the soldier, on those very plains where he himself had failed in the courage of the Christian, and so often dye with fruitless blood that very Cypriot Sea, over whose waves, in repentance and shame, he was following the Son of Consolation!

* Acts xiii. 13; xv. 38, 39.

§ II. That the Venetians possessed themselves
of his body in the ninth century, there appears
no sufficient reason to doubt, nor that it was
principally in consequence of their having done
so, that they chose him for their patron saint.[a]
The re-discovery of the relics, lost in the con-
flagration of 976, is recorded in one of the
best-preserved mosaics of the north transept,
executed very certainly not long after the event
had taken place, closely resembling in its treatment that of the Bayeux tapestry, and showing
in a conventional manner, the interior of the
church as it then was, filled by the people, first
in prayer, then in thanksgiving, the pillar
standing open before them, and the Doge, in
the midst of them, distinguished by his crimson
bonnet embroidered with gold, but more un-
mistakably by the inscription " Dux " over his
head, as uniformly is the case in the Bayeux
tapestry, and most other pictorial works of the
period. The church is, of course, rudely represented, and the two upper stories of it reduced
to a small scale in order to form a background
to the figures; one of those bold pieces of
picture history which we in our pride of perspective, and a thousand things besides,[b] never
dare attempt. The old workman has, therefore,

---

[a] [Part of the old edition (§§ 2—8) is omitted here.]

[b] [I leave this exceedingly ill-written sentence, trusting the
reader will think I write better now.]

left us some useful notes of its ancient form, though anyone who is familiar with the method of drawing employed at the period will not push the evidence too far. The two pulpits were there, however, as they are at this day, and the fringe of mosaic flower work which then encompassed the whole church, but which modern restorers have destroyed, all but one fragment still left in the south aisle. There is no attempt to represent the other mosaics on the roof, the scale being too small to admit of their being represented with any success; but some at least of those mosaics had been executed at that period, and their absence in the representation of the entire church is especially to be observed, in order to show that we must not trust to any negative evidence in such works. M. Lazari has rashly concluded that the central archivolt of St. Mark's *must* be posterior to the year 1205, because it does not appear in the representation of the exterior of the church over the northern door;* but he justly observes that this mosaic (which is the other piece of evidence we possess respecting the ancient form of the building) cannot itself be earlier than 1205, since it represents the bronze horses which were brought from Constantinople in that year. And this one fact renders it very difficult to speak with confidence respecting the date of any part of

* Lazari, 'Guida di Venezia,' p. 6. [He is right, however.]

the exterior of St. Mark's; for we have above
seen that it was consecrated in the eleventh
century, and yet here is one of its most important exterior decorations assuredly retouched,
if not entirely added, in the thirteenth, although
its style would have led us to suppose it had
been an original part of the fabric. However,
for all our purposes, it will be enough for the
reader to remember that the earliest parts of the
building belong to the eleventh, twelfth, and
first part of the thirteenth century; the Gothic
portions to the fourteenth; some of the altars
and embellishments to the fifteenth and sixteenth; and the modern portion of the mosaics
to the seventeenth.

§ IX. This, however, I only wish him to
recollect in order that I may speak generally of
the Byzantine architecture of St. Mark's without leading him to suppose the whole church to
have been built and decorated by Greek artists.
Its later portions, with the single exception of
the seventeenth century mosaics, have been so
dexterously accommodated to the original fabric
that the general effect is still that of a Byzantine
building; and I shall not, except when it is
absolutely necessary, direct attention to the
discordant points, or weary the reader with
anatomical criticism. Whatever in St. Mark's
arrests the eye, or affects the feelings, is either
Byzantine, or has been modified by Byzantine

influence; and our inquiry into its architectural merits need not therefore be disturbed by the anxieties of antiquarianism, or arrested by the obscurities of chronology.

§ x. And now I wish that the reader, before I bring him into St. Mark's Place, would imagine himself for a little time in a quiet English cathedral town, and walk with me to the west front of its cathedral. Let us go together up the more retired street, at the end of which we can see the pinnacles of one of the towers, and then through the low, grey gateway with its battlemented top and small latticed window in the centre, into the inner private-looking road or close, where nothing goes in but the carts of the tradesmen who supply the bishop and the chapter, and where there are little shaven grassplots, fenced in by neat rails, before old-fashioned groups of somewhat diminutive and excessively trim houses, with little oriel and bay windows jutting out here and there, and deep wooden cornices and eaves painted cream colour and white, and small porches to their doors in the shape of cockle-shells, or little, crooked, thick, indescribable, wooden gables warped a little on one side; and so forward till we come to larger houses, also old-fashioned, but of red brick, and with gardens behind them, and fruit walls, which show here and there, among the nectarines, the vestiges of

an old cloister arch or shaft; and looking in
front on the cathedral square itself, laid out in
rigid divisions of smooth grass and gravel walk,
yet not uncheerful, especially on the sunny side,
where the canons' children are walking with
their nurserymaids. And so, taking care not to
tread on the grass, we will go along the straight
walk to the west front, and there stand for a
time, looking up at its deep-pointed porches and
the dark places between their pillars where there
were statues once, and where the fragments,
here and there, of a stately figure are still left,
which has in it the likeness of a king, perhaps
indeed a king on earth, perhaps a saintly king
long ago in heaven; and so higher and higher
up to the great mouldering wall of rugged
sculpture and confused arcades, shattered, and
grey, and grisly with heads of dragons and
mocking fiends, worn by the rain and swirling
winds into yet unseemlier shape, and coloured
on their stony scales by the deep russet-orange
lichen,[c] melancholy gold; and so, higher still, to
the bleak towers, so far above that the eye loses
itself among the bosses of their traceries, though
they are rude and strong, and only sees, like a
drift of eddying black points, now closing, now

[c] [Alas! all this was described from things now never to
be seen more. Read, for "the great mouldering wall," and
the context of four lines, "the beautiful new parapet by
Mr. Scott, with a gross of kings sent down from Kensington."]

scattering, and now settling suddenly into invisible places among the bosses and flowers, the
crowd of restless birds that fill the whole square
with that strange clangour of theirs, so harsh
and yet so soothing, like the cries of birds on a
solitary coast between the cliffs and sea.

§ XI. Think for a little while of that scene,
and the meaning of all its small formalisms,
mixed with its serene sublimity. Estimate its
secluded, continuous, drowsy felicities, and its
evidence of the sense and steady performance of
such kind of duties as can be regulated by the
cathedral clock ; and weigh the influence of
those dark towers on all who have passed
through the lonely square at their feet for
centuries, and on all who have seen them rising
far away over the wooded plain, or catching on
their square masses the last rays of the sunset,
when the city at their feet was indicated only
by the mist at the bend of the river. And then
let us quickly recollect that we are in Venice,
and land at the extremity of the Calle Lunga
San Moisè, which may be considered as there
answering to the secluded street that led us to
our English cathedral gateway.

§ XII. We find ourselves in a paved alley,
some seven feet wide where it is widest, full of
people, and resonant with cries of itinerant
salesmen,—a shriek in their beginning, and
dying away into a kind of brazen ringing, all

the worse for its confinement between the high houses of the passage along which we have to make our way. Overhead, an inextricable confusion of rugged shutters, and iron balconies, and chimney flues, pushed out on brackets to save room, and arched windows with projecting sills of Istrian stone, and gleams of green leaves here and there, where a fig-tree branch escapes over a lower wall from some inner cortile, leading the eye up to the narrow stream of blue sky high over all. On each side, a row of shops, as densely set as may be, occupying, in fact, intervals between the square stone shafts, about eight feet high, which carry the first floors : intervals of which one is narrow and serves as a door ; the other is, in the more respectable shops, wainscoted to the height of the counter and glazed above, but in those of the poorer tradesmen left open to the ground, and the wares laid on benches and tables in the open air, the light in all cases entering at the front only, and fading away in a few feet from the threshold into a gloom which the eye from without cannot penetrate, but which is generally broken by a ray or two from a feeble lamp at the back of the shop, suspended before a print of the Virgin. The less pious shopkeeper sometimes leaves his lamp unlighted, and is contented with a penny print ; the more religious one has his print coloured and set in a little shrine with a

gilded or figured fringe, with perhaps a faded
flower or two on each side, and his lamp burning brilliantly. Here, at the fruiterer's, where
the dark-green water-melons are heaped upon
the counter like cannon-balls, the Madonna has
'a tabernacle of fresh laurel leaves; but the
pewterer next door has let his lamp out, and
there is nothing to be seen in his shop but the
dull gleam of the studded patterns on the copper
pans, hanging from his roof in the darkness.
Next comes a " Vendita Frittole e Liquori,"
where the Virgin, enthroned in a very humble
manner beside a tallow candle on a back shelf,
presides over certain ambrosial morsels of a
nature too ambiguous to be defined or enumerated. But, a few steps farther on, at the
regular wine-shop of the calle, where we are
offered " Vino Nostrani a Soldi 28·22," the
Madonna is in great glory, enthroned above ten
or a dozen large red casks of three-year-old
vintage, and flanked by goodly ranks of bottles
of Maraschino, and two crimson lamps; and
for the evening, when the gondoliers will come
to drink out, under her auspices, the money
they have gained during the day, she will have
a whole chandelier.

§ XIII. A yard or two farther, we pass the
hostelry of the Black Eagle, and glancing as we
pass through the square door of marble, deeply
moulded, in the outer wall, we see the shadows

of its pergola of vines resting on an ancient well, with a pointed shield carved on its side; and so presently emerge on the bridge and Campo San Moisè, whence to the entrance into St. Mark's Place, called the Bocca di Piazza (mouth of the square), the Venetian character is nearly destroyed, first by the frightful façade of San Moisè, which we will pause at another time to examine, and then by the modernizing of the shops as they near the piazza, and the mingling with the lower Venetian populace of lounging groups of English and Austrians. We will push fast through them into the shadow of the pillars at the end of the "Bocca di Piazza," and then we forget them all; for between those pillars there opens a great light, and, in the midst of it, as we advance slowly, the vast tower of St. Mark seems to lift itself visibly forth from the level field of chequered stones : and, on each side, the countless arches prolong themselves into ranged symmetry, as if the rugged and irregular houses that pressed together above us in the dark alley had been struck back into sudden obedience and lovely order, and all their rude casements and broken walls had been transformed into arches charged with goodly sculpture, and fluted shafts of delicate stone.

§ XIV. And well may they fall back, for beyond those troops of ordered arches there rises

a vision out of the earth, and all the great square
seems to have opened from it in a kind of awe,
that we may see it far away;—a multitude of
pillars and white domes, clustered into a long
low pyramid of coloured light; a treasure-heap
it seems, partly of gold, and partly of opal and
mother-of-pearl, hollowed beneath into five
great vaulted porches, ceiled with fair mosaic,
and beset with sculpture of alabaster, clear as
amber and delicate as ivory,—sculpture fantastic
and involved, of palm-leaves and lilies, and
grapes and pomegranates, and birds clinging and
fluttering among the branches, all twined together into an endless network of buds and
plumes; and, in the midst of it, the solemn forms
of angels, sceptred, and robed to the feet, and
leaning to each other across the gates, their
figures indistinct among the gleaming of the
golden ground through the leaves beside them,
interrupted and dim, like the morning light as
it faded back among the branches of Eden, when
first its gates were angel-guarded long ago.
And round the walls of the porches there are
set pillars of variegated stones, jasper and porphyry, and deep-green serpentine spotted with
flakes of snow, and marbles, that half refuse and
half yield to the sunshine, Cleopatra-like, "their
bluest veins to kiss,"—the shadow, as it steals
back from them, revealing line after line of
azure undulation, as a receding tide leaves the

waved sand; their capitals rich with interwoven
tracery, rooted knots of herbage, and drifting
leaves of acanthus and vine, and mystical signs,
all beginning and ending in the Cross; and
above them, in the broad archivolts, a continuous
chain of language and of life—angels, and the
signs of heaven, and the labours of men, each in
its appointed season upon the earth; and above
these, another range of glittering pinnacles,
mixed with white arches edged with scarlet
flowers,—a confusion of delight, amidst which
the breasts of the Greek horses are seen blazing
in their breadth of golden strength, and the St.
Mark's lion, lifted on a blue field covered with
stars, until at last, as if in ecstasy, the crests of
the arches break into a marble foam, and toss
themselves far into the blue sky in flashes and
wreaths of sculptured spray, as if the breakers
on the Lido shore had been frost-bound before
they fell, and the sea-nymphs had inlaid them
with coral and amethyst.

Between that grim cathedral of England and
this, what an interval! There is a type of it in
the very birds that haunt them; for, instead
of the restless crowd, hoarse-voiced and sable-
winged, drifting on the bleak upper air, the
St. Mark's porches are full of doves, that nestle
among the marble foliage, and mingle the soft
iridescence of their living plumes, changing at
every motion, with the tints, hardly less lovely,

that have stood unchanged for seven hundred years.

§ xv. And what effect has this splendour on those who pass beneath it? You may walk from sunrise to sunset, to and fro, before the gateway of St. Mark's, and you will not see an eye lifted to it, nor a countenance brightened by it. Priest and layman, soldier and civilian, rich and poor, pass by it alike regardlessly. Up to the very recesses of the porches, the meanest tradesmen of the city push their counters; nay, the foundations of its pillars are themselves the seats—not "of them that sell doves" for sacrifice, but of the vendors of toys and caricatures. Round the whole square in front of the church there is almost a continuous line of cafés, where the idle Venetians of the middle classes lounge, and read empty journals; in its centre the Austrian bands play during the time of vespers, their martial music jarring with the organ notes,—the march drowning the miserere, and the sullen crowd thickening round them,— a crowd which, if it had its will, would stiletto every soldier that pipes to it. And in the recesses of the porches, all day long, knots of men of the lowest classes, unemployed and listless, lie basking in the sun like lizards; and unregarded children,—every heavy glance of their young eyes full of desperation and stony depravity, and their throats hoarse with cursing,

—gamble, and fight, and snarl, and sleep, hour after hour, clashing their bruised centesimi upon the marble ledges of the church porch. And the images of Christ and His angels look down upon it continually.

That we may not enter the church out of the midst of the horror of this, let us turn aside under the portico which looks towards the sea, and passing round within the two massive pillars brought from St. Jean d'Acre, we shall find the gate of the Baptistery; let us enter there. The heavy door closes behind us instantly, and the light and the turbulence of the Piazzetta are together shut out by it.

§ XVI. We are in a low vaulted room; vaulted, not with arches, but with small cupolas starred with gold, and chequered with gloomy figures : in the centre is a bronze font charged with rich bas-reliefs, a small figure of the Baptist standing above it in a single ray of light that glances across the narrow room, dying as it falls from a window high in the wall, and the first thing that it strikes, and the only thing that it strikes brightly, is a tomb. We hardly know if it be a tomb indeed; for it is like a narrow couch set beside the window, low-roofed and curtained, so that it might seem, but that it is some height above the pavement, to have been drawn towards the window, that the sleeper might be wakened early; only there

are two angels who have drawn the curtain
back, and are looking down upon him. Let us
look also, and thank that gentle light that rests
upon his forehead for ever, and dies away upon
his breast.

The face is of a man, in middle life, but there
are two deep furrows right across the forehead,
dividing it like the foundations of a tower; the
height of it above is bound by the fillet of the
ducal cap. The rest of the features are singularly small and delicate, the lips sharp, perhaps
the sharpness of death being added to that of
the natural lines; but there is a sweet smile
upon them, and a deep serenity upon the whole
countenance. The roof of the canopy above
has been blue, filled with stars; beneath, in the
centre of the tomb on which the figure rests, is a
seated figure of the Virgin, and the border of it
all around is of flowers and soft leaves, growing
rich and deep, as if in a field in summer.

It is the Doge Andrea Dandolo, a man early
great among the great of Venice; and early lost.
She chose him for her king in his thirty-sixth
year; he died ten years later, leaving behind
him that history to which we owe half of what
we know of her former fortunes.

§ XVII. Look round at the room in which he
lies. The floor of it is of rich mosaic, encompassed by a low seat of red marble, and its walls
are of alabaster, but worn and shattered, and

darkly stained with age, almost a ruin,—in
places the slabs of marble have fallen away
altogether, and the rugged brickwork is seen
through the rents, but all beautiful; the ravag-
ing fissures fretting their way among the islands
and channelled zones of the alabaster, and the
time-stains on its translucent masses darkened
into fields of rich golden brown, like the colour
of seaweed when the sun strikes on it through
deep sea. The light fades away into the recess
of the chamber towards the altar, and the eye
can hardly trace the lines of the bas-relief
behind it of the baptism of Christ: but on the
vaulting of the roof the figures are distinct, and
there are seen upon it two great circles, one surrounded by the " Principalities and powers in
heavenly places," of which Milton has expressed
the ancient division in the single massy line,

" Thrones, Dominations, Princedoms, Virtues, Powers,"

and around the other, the Apostles ; Christ the
centre of both : and upon the walls, again and
again repeated, the gaunt figure of the Baptist,
in every circumstance of his life and death ; and
the streams of the Jordan running down between
their cloven rocks; the axe laid to the root of
a fruitless tree that springs upon their shore.
" Every tree that bringeth not forth good fruit
shall be hewn down, and cast into the fire."
Yes, verily : to be baptized with fire, or to be

cast therein ; it is the choice set before all men.
The march-notes still murmur through the
grated window, and mingle with the sounding
in our ears of the sentence of judgment, which
the old Greek has written on that Baptistery
wall.   Venice has made her choice.

§ XVIII.   He who lies under that stony canopy
would have taught her another choice, in his
day, if she would have listened to him ; but he
and his counsels have long been forgotten by her,
and the dust lies upon his lips.

Through the heavy door whose bronze network closes the place of his rest, let us enter the
church itself.   It is lost in still deeper twilight,
to which the eye must be accustomed for some
moments before the form of the building can be
traced ; and then there opens before us a vast
cave, hewn out into the form of a Cross, and
divided into shadowy aisles by many pillars.
Round the domes of its roof the light enters only
through narrow apertures like large stars ; and
here and there a ray or two from some far-away
casement wanders into the darkness, and casts a
narrow phosphoric stream upon the waves of
marble that heave and fall in a thousand colours
along the floor.   What else there is of light is
from torches, or silver lamps, burning ceaselessly
in the recesses of the chapels ; the roof sheeted
with gold, and the polished walls covered with
alabaster, give back at every curve and angle

some feeble gleaming to the flames; and the
glories round the heads of the sculptured saints
flash out upon us as we pass them, and sink
again into the gloom. Under foot and over
head, a continual succession of crowded imagery,
one picture passing into another, as in a dream;
forms beautiful and terrible mixed together;
dragons and serpents, and ravening beasts of
prey, and graceful birds that in the midst of
them drink from running fountains and feed
from vases of crystal; the passions and the
pleasures of human life symbolized together, and
the mystery of its redemption; for the mazes of
interwoven lines and changeful pictures lead
always at last to the Cross, lifted and carved in
every place and upon every stone; sometimes
with the serpent of eternity wrapt round it,
sometimes with doves beneath its arms, and
sweet herbage growing forth from its feet; but
conspicuous most of all on the great rood that
crosses the church before the altar, raised in
bright blazonry against the shadow of the apse.
And although in the recesses of the aisles and
chapels, when the mist of the incense hangs
heavily, we may see continually a figure traced
in faint lines upon their marble, a woman
standing with her eyes raised to heaven, and the
inscription above her, "Mother of God," she is
not here the presiding deity. It is the Cross
that is first seen, and always burning in the

centre of the temple; and every dome and hollow of its roof has the figure of Christ in the utmost height of it, raised in power, or returning in judgment.

§ XIX. Nor is this interior without effect on the minds of the people. At every hour of the day there are groups collected before the various shrines, and solitary worshippers scattered through the darker places of the church, evidently in prayer both deep and reverent, and, for the most part, profoundly sorrowful. The devotees at the greater number of the renowned shrines of Romanism may be seen murmuring their appointed prayers with wandering eyes and unengaged gestures; but the step of the stranger does not disturb those who kneel on the pavement of St. Mark's; and hardly a moment passes, from early morning to sunset, in which we may not see some half-veiled figure enter beneath the Arabian porch, cast itself into long abasement on the floor of the temple, and then rising slowly with more confirmed step, and with a passionate kiss and clasp of the arms given to the feet of the crucifix, by which the lamps burn always in the northern aisle, leave the church, as if comforted.

§ XX. But we must not hastily conclude from this that the nobler characters of the building have at present any influence in fostering a devotional spirit. There is distress enough in

Venice to bring many to their knees, without excitement from external imagery; and whatever there may be in the temper of the worship offered in St. Mark's more than can be accounted for by reference to the unhappy circumstances of the city, is assuredly not owing either to the beauty of its architecture or to the impressiveness of the Scripture histories embodied in its mosaics. That it has a peculiar effect, however slight, on the popular mind, may perhaps be safely conjectured from the number of worshippers which it attracts, while the churches of St. Paul and the Frari, larger in size and more central in position, are left comparatively empty.* But this effect is altogether to be ascribed to its richer assemblage of those sources of influence which address themselves to the commonest instincts of the human mind, and which, in all ages and countries, have been more or less employed in the support of superstition. Darkness and mystery; confused recesses of building; artificial light employed in small quantity, but maintained with a constancy which seems to give it a kind of sacredness; preciousness of material easily comprehended by the vulgar eye; close air loaded with a sweet and peculiar odour

---

* The mere warmth of St. Mark's in winter, which is much greater than that of the other two churches above named, must, however, be taken into consideration, as one of the most efficient causes of its being then more frequented.

associated only with religious services, solemn
music, and tangible idols or images having
populár legends attached to them,—these, the
stage properties of superstition, which have been
from the beginning of the world, and must be
to the end of it, employed by all nations, whether
openly savage or nominally civilized, to produce
a 'false awe in minds incapable of apprehending
the true nature of the Deity, are assembled in
St. Mark's to a degree, as far as I know, un-
exampled in any other European church. The
arts of the Magus and the Brahmin are exhausted
in the animation of a paralyzed Christianity:
and the popular sentiment which these arts
excite is to be regarded by us with no more
respect than we should have considered ourselves justified in rendering to the devotion of
the worshippers at Eleusis, Ellora, or Edfou.*

§ XXI. Indeed, these inferior means of exciting
religious emotion were employed in the ancient

---

* I said above that the larger number of the devotees
entered by the "Arabian" porch; the porch, that is to say,
on the north side of the church, remarkable for its rich
Arabian archivolt, and through which access is gained
immediately to the northern transept. The reason is that in
that transept is the chapel of the Madonna, which has a
greater attraction for the Venetians than all the rest of the
church besides. The old builders kept their images of the
Virgin subordinate to those of Christ; but modern Romanism
has retrograded from theirs, and the most glittering portions
of the whole church are the two recesses behind this lateral
altar, covered with silver hearts dedicated to the Virgin.

Church as they are at this day, but not employed alone. Torchlight there was, as there is
now; but the torchlight illumined Scripture
histories on the walls, which every eye traced
and every heart comprehended, but which, during
my whole residence in Venice, I never saw one
Venetian regard for an instant. I never heard
from any one the most languid expression of interest in any feature of the church, or perceived
the slightest evidence of their understanding the
meaning of its architecture ; and while, therefore,
the English cathedral, though no longer dedicated
to the kind of services for which it was intended
by its builders, and much at variance in many
of its characters with the temper of the people
by whom it is now surrounded, retains yet so
much of its religious influence that no prominent
feature in its architecture can be said to exist
altogether in vain, we have in St. Mark's a building apparently still employed in the ceremonies
for which it was designed, and yet of which the
impressive attributes have altogether ceased to
be comprehended by its votaries. The beauty
which it possesses is unfelt, the language it uses
is forgotten ; and in the midst of the city to
whose services it has so long been consecrated,
and still filled by crowds of the descendants of
those to whom it owes its magnificence, it stands,
in reality, more desolate than the ruins through
which the sheep-walk passes unbroken in our

English valleys; and the writing on its marble walls is less regarded and less powerful for the teaching of men, than the letters which the shepherd follows with his finger, where the moss is lightest on the tombs in the desecrated cloister.

§ XXII. It must therefore be altogether without reference to its present usefulness, that we pursue our inquiry into the merits and meaning of the architecture of this marvellous building; and it can only be after we have terminated that inquiry, conducting it carefully on abstract grounds, that we can pronounce with any certainty how far the present neglect of St. Mark's is significative of the decline of the Venetian character, or how far this church is to be considered as the relic of a barbarous age, incapable of attracting the admiration, or influencing the feelings, of a civilized community.

The inquiry before us is twofold. Throughout the first volume, I carefully kept the study of *expression* distinct from that of abstract architectural perfection; telling the reader that in every building we should afterwards examine, he would have first to form a judgment of its construction and decorative merit, considering it merely as a work of art; and then to examine farther, in what degree it fulfilled its expressional purposes. Accordingly, we have first to judge of St. Mark's merely as a piece of architecture,

not as a church ; secondly, to estimate its fitness
for its special duty as a place of worship, and the
relation in which it stands, as such, to those
Northern cathedrals that still retain so much
of the power over the human heart, which the
Byzantine domes appear to have lost for ever.

§ XXIII. In the two succeeding sections of this
work, devoted respectively to the examination
of the Gothic and Renaissance buildings in
Venice, I have endeavoured to analyze, and state
as briefly as possible, the true nature of each
school,—first in Spirit, then in Form. I wished
to have given a similar analysis, in this section, of
the nature of Byzantine architecture ; but could
not make my statements general, because I have
never seen this kind of building on its native
soil. Nevertheless, in the following sketch of
the principles exemplified in St. Mark's, I believe
that most of the leading features and motives of
the style will be found clearly enough distinguished to enable the reader to judge of it with
tolerable fairness, as compared with the better
known systems of European architecture in the
middle ages.

§ XXIV. Now the first broad characteristic of
the building, and the root nearly of every other
important peculiarity in it, is its confessed *incrustation*. It is the purest example in Italy of
the great school of architecture in which the
ruling principle is the incrustation of brick with

more precious materials; and it is necessary,
before we proceed to criticise any one of its
arrangements, that the reader should carefully
consider the principles which are likely to have
influenced, or might legitimately influence, the
architects of such a school, as distinguished from
those whose designs are to be executed in massive
materials.

It is true, that among different nations, and at
different times, we may find examples of every
sort and degree of incrustation, from the mere
setting of the larger and more compact stones
by preference at the outside of the wall, to the
miserable construction of that modern brick
cornice with its coating of cement, which, but
the other day in London, killed its unhappy
workmen in its fall.* But just as it is perfectly
possible to have a clear idea of opposing the
characteristics of two different species of plants
or animals, though between the two there are
varieties which it is difficult to assign either to
the one or the other, so the reader may fix
decisively in his mind the legitimate characteristics of the incrusted and the massive styles,
though between the two there are varieties which
confessedly unite the attributes of both.   For
instance, in many Roman remains, built of blocks
of tufa and incrusted with marble, we have a
style which, though truly solid, possesses some

* Vide ' Builder' for October, 1851.

of the attributes of incrustation; and in the
Cathedral of Florence, built of brick and coated
with marble, the marble facing is so firmly
and exquisitely set, that the building, though
in reality incrusted, assumes the attributes of
solidity. But these intermediate examples need
not in the least confuse our generally distinct
ideas of the two families of buildings : the one in
which the substance is alike throughout, and the
forms and conditions of the ornament assume or
prove that it is so, as in the best Greek buildings,
and for the most part in our early Norman and
Gothic ; and the other, in which the substance is
of two kinds, one internal, the other external,
and the system of decoration is founded on this
duplicity, as pre-eminently in St. Mark's.

§ xxv. I have used the word duplicity in
no depreciatory sense. In Chapter II. of the
' Seven Lamps,' § 18, I especially guarded this
incrusted school from the imputation of insin-
cerity, and I must do so now at greater length.
It appears insincere at first to a Northern builder,
because, accustomed to build with solid blocks
of freestone, he is in the habit of supposing the
external superficies of a piece of masonry to be
some criterion of its thickness. But, as soon as
he gets acquainted with the incrusted style, he
will find that the Southern builders had no intention to deceive him. He will see that every
slab of facial marble is fastened to the next by a

confessed *rivet*, and that the joints of the armour
are so visibly and openly accommodated to the
contours of the substance within, that he has no
more right to complain of treachery than a savage
would have, who, for the first time in his life
seeing a man in armour, had supposed him to
be made of solid steel. Acquaint him with the
customs of chivalry, and with the uses of the
coat of mail, and he ceases to accuse of dishonesty either the panoply or the knight.

These laws and customs of the St. Mark's
architectural chivalry it must be our business to
develop.

§ XXVI. First, consider the natural circumstances which give rise to such a style. Suppose
a nation of builders, placed far from any quarries
of available stone, and having precarious access
to the mainland where they exist; compelled
therefore either to build entirely with brick, or to
import whatever stone they use from great distances, in ships of small tonnage, and for the most
part dependent for speed on the oar rather than
the sail. The labour and cost of carriage are just
as great, whether they import common or precious
stone, and therefore the natural tendency would
always be to make each shipload as valuable as
possible. But in proportion to the preciousness
of the stone, is the limitation of its possible
supply; limitation not determined merely by
cost, but by the physical conditions of the

material, for of many marbles pieces above a certain size are not to be had for money.   There
would also be a tendency in such circumstances
to import as much stone as possible ready
sculptured, in order to save weight; and therefore, if the traffic of their merchants led them to
places where there were ruins of ancient edifices,
to ship the available fragments of them home.
Out of this supply of marble, partly composed of
pieces of so precious a quality that only a few
tons of them could be on any terms obtained,
and partly of shafts, capitals, and other portions
of foreign buildings, the island architect has to
fashion, as best he may, the anatomy of his
edifice.   It is at his choice either to lodge his few
blocks of precious marble here and there among
his masses of brick, and to cut out of the sculptured fragments such new forms as may be necessary for the observance of fixed proportions in
the new building; or else to cut the coloured
stones into thin pieces, of extent sufficient to face
the whole surface of the walls, and to adopt a
method of construction irregular enough to admit
the insertion of fragmentary sculptures; rather
with a view of displaying their intrinsic beauty,
than of setting them to any regular service in the
support of the building.

An architect who cared only to display his own
skill, and had no respect for the works of others,
would assuredly have chosen the former alternative,

and would have sawn the old marbles into fragments in order to prevent all interference with
his own designs.   But an architect who cared for
the preservation of noble work, whether his own
or others', and more regarded the beauty of his
building than his own fame, would have done what
those old builders of St. Mark's did for us, and
saved every relic with which he was entrusted.

§ XXVII. But these were not the only motives
which influenced the Venetians in the adoption
of their method of architecture. It might, under
all the circumstances above stated, have been a
question with other builders, whether to import
one shipload of costly jaspers, or twenty of chalk
flints ; and whether to build a small church faced
with porphyry and paved with agate, or to raise
a vast cathedral in freestone.   But with the
Venetians it could not be a question for an
instant ; they were exiles from ancient and beautiful cities, and had been accustomed to build
with their ruins, not less in affection than in admiration : they had thus not only grown familiar
with the practice of inserting older fragments
in modern buildings, but they owed to that
practice a great part of the splendour of their
city, and whatever charm of association might
aid its change from a Refuge into a Home.   The
practice which began in the affections of a fugitive
nation, was prolonged in the pride of a conquering one ; and beside the memorials of departed

happiness, were elevated the trophies of returning victory. The ship of war brought home more marble in triumph than the merchant vessel in speculation; and the front of St. Mark's became rather a shrine at which to dedicate the splendour of miscellaneous spoil, than the organized expression of any fixed architectural law or religious emotion.

§ XXVIII. Thus far, however, the justification of the style of this church depends on circumstances peculiar to the time of its erection, and to the spot where it arose. The merit of its method, considered in the abstract, rests on far broader grounds.

In the fifth chapter of the 'Seven Lamps,' § 14, the reader will find the opinion of a modern architect of some reputation, Mr. Wood, that the chief thing remarkable in this church "is its extreme ugliness;" and he will find this opinion associated with another, namely, that the works of the Caracci are far preferable to those of the Venetian painters. The second statement of feeling reveals to us one of the principal causes of the first; namely, that Mr. Wood had not any perception of colour or delight in it. The perception of colour is a gift just as definitely granted to one person, and denied to another, as an ear for music; and the very first requisite for true judgment of St. Mark's, is the perfection of that colour-faculty which few people ever set

themselves seriously to find out whether they
possess or not. For it is on its value as a piece
of perfect and unchangeable colouring, that the
claims of this edifice to our respect are finally
rested ; and a deaf man might as well pretend
to pronounce judgment on the merits of a full
orchestra, as an architect trained in the composition of form only, to discern the beauty of
St. Mark's. It possesses the charm of colour in
common with the greater part of the architecture,
as well as of the manufactures, of the East; but
the Venetians deserve especial note as the only
European people who appear to have sympathised
to the full with the great instinct of the Eastern
races. They indeed were compelled to bring
artists from Constantinople to design the mosaics
of the vaults of St. Mark's and to group the
colours of its porches ; but they rapidly took up
and developed, under more masculine conditions,
the system of which the Greeks had shown them
the example : while the burghers and barons of
the North were building their dark streets and
grisly castles of oak and sandstone, the merchants
of Venice were covering their palaces with porphyry and gold ; and at last, when her mighty
painters had created for her a colour more priceless than gold or porphyry, even this, the richest
of her treasures, she lavished upon walls whose
foundations were beaten by the sea ; and the
strong tide, as it runs beneath the Rialto, is

reddened to this day by the reflection of the frescoes of Giorgione.

§ XXIX. If, therefore, the reader does not care for colour, I must protest against his endeavour to form any judgment whatever of this church of St. Mark's. But if he both cares for and loves it, let him remember that the school of incrusted architecture is *the only one in which perfect and permanent chromatic decoration is possible;* and let him look upon every piece of jasper and alabaster given to the architect as a cake of very hard colour, of which a certain portion is to be ground down or cut off, to paint the walls with. Once understand this thoroughly, and accept the condition that the body and availing strength of the edifice are to be in brick, and that this under muscular power of brickwork is to be clothed with the defence of the brightness of the marble, as the body of an animal is protected and adorned by its scales or its skin, and all the consequent fitnesses and laws of the structure will be easily discernible. These I shall state in their natural order.

§ XXX. LAW I. *That the plinths and cornices used for binding the armour are to be light and delicate.* A certain thickness, at least two or three inches, must be required in the covering pieces (even when composed of the strongest stone, and set on the least exposed parts), in order to prevent the chance of fracture, and to allow

for the wear of time. And the weight of this
armour must not be trusted to cement; the pieces
must not be merely glued to the rough brick
surface, but connected with the mass which they
protect by binding cornices and string courses,
and with each other, so as to secure mutual support, aided by the rivetings, but by no means
dependent upon them. And, for the full honesty
and straightforwardness of the work, it is necessary that these string courses and binding plinths
should not be of such proportions as would fit
them for taking any important part in the hard
work of the inner structure, or render them liable
to be mistaken for the great cornices and plinths
already explained as essential parts of the best
solid building. They must be delicate, slight,
and visibly incapable of severer work than that
assigned to them.

§ xxxi. Law II. *Science of inner structure is
to be abandoned.* As the body of the structure
is confessedly of inferior, and comparatively in-
coherent materials, it would be absurd to attempt
in it any expression of the higher refinements of
construction. It will be enough that by its mass
we are assured of its sufficiency and strength;
and there is the less reason for endeavouring to
diminish the extent of its surface by delicacy of
adjustment, because on the breadth of that surface we are to depend for the better display of
the colour, which is to be the chief source of our

pleasure in the building. The main body of the work, therefore, will be composed of solid walls and massive piers; and whatever expression of finer structural science we may require, will be thrown either into subordinate portions of it, or entirely directed to the support of the external mail, where in arches or vaults it might otherwise appear dangerously independent of the material within.

§ XXXII. LAW III. *All shafts are to be solid.* Wherever, by the smallness of the parts, we may be driven to abandon the incrusted structure at all, it must be abandoned altogether. The eye must never be left in the least doubt as to what is solid and what is coated. Whatever appears *probably* solid must be *assuredly* so, and therefore it becomes an inviolable law that no shaft shall ever be incrusted. Not only does the whole virtue of a shaft depend on its consolidation, but the labour of cutting and adjusting an incrusted coat to it would be greater than the saving of material is worth. Therefore the shaft, of whatever size, is always to be solid; and because the incrusted character of the rest of the building renders it more difficult for the shafts to clear themselves from suspicion, they must not, in this incrusted style, be in any place jointed. No shaft must ever be used but of one block; and this the more, because the permission given to the builder to have his walls and piers as ponderous as he likes, renders it quite unnecessary for him to use

shafts of any fixed size. In our Norman and
Gothic, where definite support is required at a
definite point, it becomes lawful to build up a
tower of small stones in the shape of a shaft. But
the Byzantine is allowed to have as much support as he wants from the walls in every direction, and he has no right to ask for further license
in the structure of his shafts. Let him, by
generosity in the substance of his pillars, repay
us for the permission we have given him to be
superficial in his walls. The builder in the chalk
valleys of France and England may be blameless
in kneading his clumsy pier out of broken flint
and calcined lime; but the Venetian, who has
access to the riches of Asia and the quarries
of Egypt, must frame at least his shafts out
of flawless stone.

§ XXXIII. And this for another reason yet.
Although, as we have said, it is impossible to
cover the walls of a large building with colour,
except on the condition of dividing the stone into
plates, there is always a certain appearance of
meanness and niggardliness in the procedure. It
is necessary that the builder should justify himself from this suspicion; and prove that it is not
in mere economy or poverty, but in the real impossibility of doing otherwise, that he has sheeted
his walls so thinly with the precious film. Now
the shaft is exactly the portion of the edifice in
which it is fittest to recover his honour in this

respect. For if blocks of jasper or porphyry be
inserted in the walls, the spectator cannot tell
their thickness, and cannot judge of the costliness
of the sacrifice. But the shaft he can measure
with his eye in an instant, and estimate the
quantity of treasure both in the mass of its existing substance, and in that which has been hewn
away to bring it into its perfect and symmetrical
form. And thus the shafts of all buildings of
this kind are justly regarded as an expression of
their wealth, and a form of treasure, just as much
as the jewels or gold in the sacred vessels ; they
are, in fact, nothing else than large jewels,* the
block of precious serpentine or jasper being
valued according to its size and brilliancy of
colour, like a large emerald or ruby ; only the
bulk required to bestow value on the one is to
be measured in feet and tons, and on the other in
lines and carats. The shafts must therefore be,
without exception, of one block in all buildings
of this kind ; for the attempt in any place to in-
crust or joint them would be a deception like that
of introducing a false stone among jewellery (for
a number of joints of any precious stone are of
course not equal in value to a single piece of
equal weight), and would put an end at once to
the spectator's confidence in the expression of

* "Quivi presso si vedi una colonna di tanta bellezza e
finezza che e riputato *piutosto gioia che pietra.*"—*Sansovino,*
of the verd-antique pillar in San Jacomo dell' Orio.

wealth in any portion of the structure, or of the spirit of sacrifice in those who raised it.

§ XXXIV. LAW IV. *The shafts may sometimes be independent of the construction.* Exactly in proportion to the importance which the shaft assumes as a large jewel, is the diminution of its importance as a sustaining member ; for the delight which we receive in its abstract bulk, and beauty of colour, is altogether independent of any perception of its adaptation to mechanical necessities. Like other beautiful things in this world, its end is to *be* beautiful; and, in proportion to its beauty, it receives permission to be otherwise useless. We do not blame emeralds and rubies because we cannot make them into heads of hammers. Nay, so far from our admiration of the jewel shaft being dependent on its doing work for us, it is very possible that a chief part of its preciousness may consist in a delicacy, fragility, and tenderness of material which must render it utterly unfit for hard work; and therefore that we shall admire it the more, because we perceive that if we were to put much weight upon it, it would be crushed. But, at all events, it is very clear that the primal object in the placing of such shafts must be the display of their beauty to the best advantage, and that therefore all imbedding of them in walls, or crowding of them into groups, in any position in which either their real size or any portion of their surface would be concealed, is either inadmissible altogether, or objectionable in proportion to their value; that no symmetrical or scientific arrangement of pillars is therefore ever to be expected in buildings of this kind, and that all such are even to be looked upon as positive errors and misapplications of materials: but that, on the contrary, we must be constantly prepared to see, and to see with admiration, shafts of great size and importance set in places where their real service is little more than nominal, and where the chief end of their existence is to catch the sunshine upon their polished sides, and lead the eye into delighted wandering among the mazes of their azure veins.

§ XXXV. LAW V. *The shafts may be of variable size.* Since the value of each shaft depends upon its bulk, and diminishes with the diminution of its mass in a greater ratio than the size itself diminishes, as in the case of all other jewellery, it is evident that we must not in general expect perfect symmetry and equality among the series of shafts, any more than definiteness of application; but that, on the contrary, an accurately observed symmetry ought to give us a kind of pain, as proving that considerable and useless loss has been sustained by some of the shafts, in being cut down to match with the rest. It is true that symmetry is generally sought for in works of smaller jewellery; but, even there, not a perfect symmetry, and obtained under circumstances quite different from those which affect the placing of shafts in architecture. First: the symmetry is usually imperfect. The stones that seem to match each other in a ring or necklace, appear to do so only because they are so small that their differences are not easily measured by the eye; but there is almost always such difference between them as would be strikingly apparent if it existed in the same proportion between two shafts nine or ten feet in height. Secondly: the quantity of stones which pass through a jeweller's hands, and the facility of exchange of such small objects, enable the tradesman to select any number of stones of approximate size; a selection, however, often requiring so much time, that perfect symmetry in a group of very fine stones adds enormously to their value. But the architect has neither the time nor the facilities of exchange. He cannot lay aside one column in a corner of his church till, in the course of traffic, he obtain another that will match it; he has not hundreds of shafts fastened up in bundles, out of which he can match sizes at his ease; he cannot send to a brother tradesman and exchange the useless stones for available ones, to the convenience of both. His blocks of stone, or his ready hewn shafts, have been brought to him in limited number, from immense distances; no others are to be had; and for those which he does not bring into use,

there is no demand elsewhere. His only means
of obtaining symmetry will therefore be, in
cutting down the finer masses to equality with
the inferior ones; and this we ought not to desire
him often to do. And therefore, while sometimes
in a Baldacchino, or an important chapel or shrine,
this costly symmetry may be necessary, and admirable in proportion to its probable cost, in the
general fabric we must expect to see shafts introduced of size and proportion continually varying,
and such symmetry as may be obtained among
them never altogether perfect, and dependent for
its charm frequently on strange complexities and
unexpected rising and falling of weight and accent
in its marble syllables : bearing the same relation
to a rigidly chiselled and proportioned architecture that the wild lyric rhythm of Æschylus or
Pindar bears to the finished measures of Pope.

§ XXXVI. The application of the principles of
jewellery to the smaller as well as the larger
blocks, will suggest to us another reason for the
method of incrustation adopted in the walls. It
often happens that the beauty of the veining in
some varieties of alabaster is so great, that it
becomes desirable to exhibit it by dividing the
stone, not merely to economise its substance, but
to display the changes in the disposition of its
fantastic lines. By reversing one of two thin
plates successively taken from the stone, and
placing their corresponding edges in contact, a

perfectly symmetrical figure may be obtained,
which will enable the eye to comprehend more
thoroughly the position of the veins. And this
is actually the method in which, for the most
part, the alabasters of St. Mark's are employed;
thus accomplishing a double good,—directing the
spectator, in the first place, to close observation
of the nature of the stone employed, and, in the
second, giving him a farther proof of the honesty
of intention in the builder : for wherever similar
veining is discovered in two pieces, the fact is
declared that they have been cut from the same
stone. It would have been easy to disguise the
similarity by using them in different parts of the
building; but on the contrary they are set edge
to edge, so that the whole system of the architecture may be discovered at a glance by any one
acquainted with the nature of the stones employed. Nay, but, it is perhaps answered me,
not by an ordinary observer; a person ignorant
of the nature of alabaster might perhaps fancy all
these symmetrical patterns to have been found
in the stone itself, and thus be doubly deceived,
supposing blocks to be solid and symmetrical
which were in reality subdivided and irregular.
I grant it; but be it remembered, that in all
things, ignorance is liable to be deceived, and
has no right to accuse anything but itself as
the source of the deception. The style and the
words are dishonest, not which are liable to be

misunderstood if subjected to no inquiry, but which are deliberately calculated to lead inquiry astray.

There are perhaps no great or noble truths, from those of religion downwards, which present no mistakable aspect to casual or ignorant contemplation. Both the truth and the lie agree in hiding themselves at first, but the lie continues to hide itself with effort, as we approach to examine it; and leads us, if undiscovered, into deeper lies: the truth reveals itself in proportion to our patience and knowledge, discovers itself kindly to our pleading, and leads us, as it is discovered, into deeper truths.

§ XXXVII. LAW VI. *The decoration must be shallow in cutting.* The method of construction being thus systematized, it is evident that a certain style of decoration must arise out of it, based on the primal condition that over the greater part of the edifice there can be *no deep cutting.* The thin sheets of covering stones do not admit of it; we must not cut them through to the bricks; and whatever ornaments we engrave upon them cannot, therefore, be more than an inch deep at the utmost. Consider for an instant the enormous differences which this single condition compels between the sculptural decoration of the incrusted style, and that of the solid stones of the North, which may be hacked and hewn into whatever cavernous hollows and black recesses we choose; struck into grim

darknesses and grotesque projections, and rugged ploughings up of sinuous furrows, in which
any form or thought may be wrought out on
any scale,—mighty statues with robes of rock
and crowned foreheads burning in the sun, or
venomous goblins and stealthy dragons shrunk
into lurking-places of untraceable shade : think
of this, and of the play and freedom given to the
sculptor's hand and temper, to smite out and in,
hither and thither, as he will; and then consider
what must be the different spirit of the design
which is to be wrought on the smooth surface
of a film of marble, where every line and shadow
must be drawn with the most tender pencilling
and cautious reserve of resource,—where even the
chisel must not strike hard, lest it break through
the delicate stone, nor the mind be permitted in
any impetuosity of conception inconsistent with
the fine discipline of the hand. Consider that
whatever animal or human form is to be suggested, must be projected on a flat surface ; that
all the features of the countenance, the folds of
the drapery, the involutions of the limbs, must be
so reduced and subdued that the whole work
becomes rather a piece of fine drawing than of
sculpture : and then follow out, until you begin
to perceive their endlessness, the resulting differences of character which will be necessitated
in every part of the ornamental designs of these
incrusted churches, as compared with that of the

Northern schools. I shall endeavour to trace a few of them only.

§ XXXVIII. The first would of course be a diminution of the builder's dependence upon human form as a source of ornament: since exactly in proportion to the dignity of the form itself is the loss which it must sustain in being reduced to a shallow and linear bas-relief, as well as the difficulty of expressing it at all under such conditions. Wherever sculpture can be solid, the nobler characters of the human form at once lead the artist to aim at its representation, rather than at that of inferior organisms; but when all is to be reduced to outline, the forms of flowers and lower animals are always more intelligible, and are felt to approach much more to a satisfactory rendering of the objects intended, than the outlines of the human body. This inducement to seek for resources of ornament in the lower fields of creation was powerless in the minds of the great Pagan nations, Ninevite, Greek, or Egyptian; first, because their thoughts were so concentrated on their own capacities and fates, that they preferred the rudest suggestion of human form to the best of an inferior organism; secondly, because their constant practice in solid sculpture, often colossal, enabled them to bring a vast amount of science into the treatment of the lines, whether of the low relief, the monochrome vase, or shallow hieroglyphic.

§ xxxix. But when various ideas adverse to
the representation of animal, and especially of
human, form, originating with the Arabs and
iconoclast Greeks, had begun at any rate to
direct the builders' minds to seek for decorative
materials in inferior types, and when diminished
practice in solid sculpture had rendered it more
difficult to find artists capable of satisfactorily
reducing the high organisms to their elementary
outlines, the choice of subject for surface sculpture would be more and more uninterruptedly
directed to floral organisms, and human and
animal form would become diminished in size,
frequency, and general importance. So that,
while in the Northern solid architecture we
constantly find the effect of its noblest features
dependent on ranges of statues, often colossal,
and full of abstract interest, independent of their
architectural service, in the Southern incrusted
style we must expect to find the human form for
the most part subordinate and diminutive, and
involved among designs of foliage and flowers, in
the manner of which endless examples had been
furnished by the fantastic ornamentation of the
Romans, from which the incrusted style had
been directly derived.

§ xl. Farther. In proportion to the degree
in which his object must be reduced to abstract
outline will be the tendency in the sculptor
to abandon naturalism of representation, and

subordinate every form to architectural service.
When the flower or animal can be hewn into
bold relief, there will always be a temptation to
render the representation of it more complete
than is necessary, or even to introduce details
and intricacies inconsistent with simplicity of
distant effect. Very often a worse fault than
this is committed; and in the endeavour to give
vitality to the stone, the original ornamental
purpose of the design is sacrificed or forgotten.
But when nothing of this kind can be attempted,
and a slight outline is all that the sculptor can
command, we may anticipate that this outline
will be composed with exquisite grace; and that
the richness of its ornamental arrangement will
atone for the feebleness of its power of portraiture. On the porch of a Northern cathedral
we may seek for the images of the flowers that
grow in the neighbouring fields, and as we watch
with wonder the grey stones that fret themselves
into thorns, and soften into blossoms, we may
care little that these knots of ornament, as we
retire from them to contemplate the whole building, appear unconsidered or confused. On the
incrusted building we must expect no such
deception of the eye or thoughts. It may
sometimes be difficult to determine, from the
involutions of its linear sculpture, what were
the natural forms which originally suggested
them : but we may confidently expect that the

grace of their arrangement will always be complete ; that there will not be a line in them which could be taken away without injury, nor one wanting which could be added with advantage.

§ XLI. Farther. While the sculptures of the incrusted school will thus be generally distinguished by care and purity rather than force, and will be for the most part utterly wanting in depth of shadow, there will be one means of obtaining darkness peculiarly simple and obvious, and often in the sculptor's power. Wherever he can, without danger, leave a hollow behind his covering slabs, or use them, like glass, to fill an aperture in the wall, he can, by piercing them with holes, obtain points or spaces of intense blackness to contrast with the light tracing of the rest of his design. And we may expect to find this artifice used the more extensively, because, while it will be an effective means of ornamentation on the exterior of the building, it will be also the safest way of admitting light to the interior, still totally excluding both rain and wind. And it will naturally follow that the architect, thus familiarized with the effect of black and sudden points of shadow, will often seek to carry the same principle into other portions of his ornamentation, and by deep drill-holes, or perhaps inlaid portions of black colour, to refresh the eye where it may be wearied by the lightness of the general handling.

§ XLII. Farther. Exactly in proportion to the degree in which the force of sculpture is subdued, will be the importance attached to colour as a means of effect or constituent of beauty. I have above stated that the incrusted style was the only one in which perfect or permanent colour decoration was *possible*. It is also the only one in which a true system of colour decoration was ever likely to be invented. In order to understand this, the reader must permit me to review with some care the nature of the principles of colouring adopted by the Northern and Southern nations.

§ XLIII. I believe that from the beginning of the world there has never been a true or fine school of art in which colour was despised. It has often been imperfectly attained and injudiciously applied, but I believe it to be one of the essential signs of life in a school of art, that it loves colour; and I know it to be one of the first signs of death in the Renaissance schools, that they despised colour.

Observe, it is not now the question whether our Northern cathedrals are better with colour or without. Perhaps the great monotone grey of Nature and of time is a better colour than any that the human hand can give; but that is nothing to our present business. The simple fact is, that the builders of those cathedrals laid upon them the brightest colours they could obtain, and that there is not, as far as I am aware, in Europe, any monument of a truly noble school which has not been either painted all over, or vigorously touched with paint, mosaic, and gilding in its prominent parts. Thus far, Egyptians, Greeks, Goths, Arabs, and mediæval Christians all agree : none of them, when in their right senses, ever think of doing without paint; and, therefore, when I said above that the Venetians were the only people who had thoroughly sympathized with the Arabs in this respect, I referred, first to their intense love of colour, which led them to lavish the most expensive decorations on ordinary dwelling-houses; and, secondly, to that perfection of the colour-instinct in them, which enabled them to render whatever they did, in this kind, as just in principle as it was gorgeous in appliance. It is this principle of theirs, as distinguished from that of the Northern builders, which we have finally to examine.

§ XLIV. In the second chapter of the first volume,* it was noticed that the architect of Bourges Cathedral liked hawthorn, and that the porch of his cathedral was therefore decorated with a rich wreath of it; but another of the predilections of that architect was there unnoticed, namely, that he did not at all like *grey* hawthorn, but preferred it green, and he painted it

* (Of the old edition.)

green accordingly, as bright as he could. The colour is still left in every sheltered interstice of the foliage. He had, in fact, hardly the choice of any other colour; he might have gilded the thorns, by way of allegorizing human life, but if they were to be painted at all, they could hardly be painted anything but green, and green all over. People would have been apt to object to any pursuit of abstract harmonies of colour which might have induced him to paint his hawthorn blue.

§ XLV. In the same way, whenever the subject of the sculpture was definite, its colour was of necessity definite also; and, in the hands of the Northern builders, it often became, in consequence, rather the means of explaining and animating the stories of their stone-work, than a matter of abstract decorative science. Flowers were painted red, trees green, and faces flesh-colour: the result of the whole being often far more entertaining than beautiful. And also, though in the lines of the mouldings and the decorations of shafts or vaults, a richer and more abstract method of colouring was adopted (aided by the rapid development of the best principles of colour in early glass-painting), the vigorous depths of shadow in the Northern sculpture confused the architect's eye, compelling him to use violent colours in the recesses, if these were to be seen as colour at all, and thus injured his

perception of more delicate colour harmonies; so
that in innumerable instances it becomes very
disputable whether monuments even of the best
times were improved by the colour bestowed
upon them, or the contrary. But, in the South,
the flatness and comparatively vague forms of
the sculpture, while they appeared to call for
colour in order to enhance their interest, presented exactly the conditions which would set it
off to the greatest advantage; breadth of surface
displaying even the most delicate tints in the
lights, and faintness of shadow joining with the
most delicate and pearly greys of colour harmony;
while the subject of the design being in nearly
all cases reduced to mere intricacy of ornamental
line, might be coloured in any way the architect
chose without any loss of rationality.   Where oak-
leaves and roses were carved into fresh relief and
perfect bloom, it was necessary to paint the one
green and the other red; but in portions of ornamentation where there was nothing which could
be definitely construed into either an oak-leaf or
a rose, but a mere labyrinth of beautiful lines,
becoming here something like a leaf, and there
something like a flower, the whole tracery of the
sculpture might be left white, and grounded with
gold or blue, or treated in any other manner best
harmonizing with the colours around it.   And
as the necessarily feeble character of the sculpture called for, and was ready to display, the

best arrangements of colour, so the precious marbles in the architect's hands give him at once the best examples and the best means of colour. The best examples, for the tints of all natural stones, are as exquisite in quality as endless in change; and the best means, for they are all permanent.

§ XLVI. Every motive thus concurred in urging him to the study of chromatic decoration, and every advantage was given him in the pursuit of it; and this at the very moment when, as presently to be noticed, *naïveté* of barbaric Christianity could only be forcibly appealed to by the help of coloured pictures: so that, both externally and internally, the architectural construction became partly merged in pictorial effect; and the whole edifice is to be regarded less as a temple wherein to pray, than as itself a Book of Common Prayer, a vast illuminated missal, bound with alabaster instead of parchment, studded with porphyry pillars instead of jewels, and written within and without in letters of enamel and gold.

§ XLVII. LAW VII. *That the impression of the architecture is not to be dependent on size.* And now there is but one final consequence to be deduced. The reader understands, I trust, by this time, that the claims of these several parts of the building upon his attention will depend upon their delicacy of design, their perfection

of colour, their preciousness of material, and
their legendary interest.   All these qualities
are independent of size, and partly even inconsistent with it.   Neither delicacy of surface
sculpture, nor subtle gradations of colour, can
be appreciated by the eye at a distance; and
since we have seen that our sculpture is generally
to be only an inch or two in depth, and that our
colouring is in great part to be produced with
the soft tints and veins of natural stones, it will
follow necessarily that none of the parts of the
building can be removed far from the eye, and
therefore that the whole mass of it cannot be
large.   It is not even desirable that it should be
so; for the temper in which the mind addresses
itself to contemplate minute and beautiful details is altogether different from that in which it
submits itself to vague impressions of space and
size.   And therefore we must not be disappointed, but grateful, when we find all the best
work of the building concentrated within a space
comparatively small; and that, for the great
cliff-like buttresses and mighty piers of the
North shooting up into indiscernible height,
we have here low walls spread before us like
the pages of a book, and shafts whose capitals
we may touch with our hand.

§ XLVIII. The due consideration of the principles above stated will enable the traveller to
judge with more candour and justice of the

architecture of St. Mark's than usually it would have been possible for him to do while under the influence of the prejudices necessitated by familiarity with the very different schools of Northern art. I wish it were in my power to lay also before the general reader some exemplification of the manner in which these strange principles are developed in the lovely building. But exactly in proportion to the nobility of any work, is the difficulty of conveying a just impression of it; and wherever I have occasion to bestow high praise, there it is exactly most dangerous for me to endeavour to illustrate my meaning, except by reference to the work itself. And, in fact, the principal reason why architectural criticism is at this day so far behind all other, is the impossibility of illustrating the best architecture faithfully. Of the various schools of painting, examples are accessible to every one, and reference to the works themselves is found sufficient for all purposes of criticism; but there is nothing like St. Mark's or the Ducal Palace to be referred to in the National Gallery, and no faithful illustration of them is possible on the scale of such a volume as this. And it is exceedingly difficult on any scale. Nothing is so rare in art, as far as my own experience goes, as a fair illustration of architecture; *perfect* illustration of it does not exist. For all good architecture depends upon the adaptation of its chiselling

to the effect at a certain distance from the eye;
and to render the peculiar confusion in the midst
of order, and uncertainty in the midst of decision,
and mystery in the midst of trenchant lines,
which are the result of distance, together with
perfect expression of the peculiarities of the
design, requires the skill of the most admirable
artist, devoted to the work with the most severe
conscientiousness; neither the skill nor the determination having as yet been given to the subject.
And in the illustration of details, every building
of any pretensions to high architectural rank
would require a volume of plates, and those
finished with extraordinary care.   With respect
to the two buildings which are the principal subjects of the present volume, St. Mark's and the
Ducal Palace, I have found it quite impossible
to do them the slightest justice by any kind
of portraiture.   As for St. Mark's, the effort was
hopeless from the beginning.   For its effects depend
not only upon the most delicate sculpture in every
part, but, as we have just stated, eminently on
its colour also, and that the most subtle, variable,
inexpressible colour in the world,—the colour of
glass, of transparent alabaster, of polished marble,
and lustrous gold.   It would be easier to illustrate
a crest of Scottish mountain, with its purple
heather and pale harebells at their fullest and
fairest, or a glade of Jura forest, with its floor
of anemone and moss, than a single portico of

St. Mark's.* The fragment of one of its archivolts, given at the bottom of the opposite
photograph,° is not to illustrate the thing
itself, but to illustrate the impossibility of
illustration.

§ XLIX. It is left a fragment, in order to get
it on a larger scale; and yet even on this scale it
is too small to show the sharp folds and points
of the marble vine-leaves with sufficient clearness.
The ground of it is gold, the sculpture in the
spandrils is not more than half an inch deep,
rarely so much. It is in fact nothing more
than an exquisite sketching of outlines in marble
to about the same depth as in the Elgin frieze;
the draperies, however, being filled with close
folds, in the manner of the Byzantine pictures,
folds especially necessary here, as large masses
could not be expressed in the shallow sculpture
without becoming insipid; but the disposition
of these folds is always most beautiful, and often
opposed by broad and simple spaces, like that
obtained by the scroll in the hand of the figure.

The balls in the archivolt project considerably,
and the interstices between their interwoven
bands of marble are filled with colours like the

* The two loveliest of which have now been torn down, and
vile models put up where they stood, by the accursed modern
Italians.

° [See preface, for my present system of illustration, and
directions to binder. The portico is the one on left hand of
great entrance, and may best be examined to illustrate itself.]

illuminations of a manuscript; violet, crimson, blue, gold, and green, alternately : but no green is ever used without an intermixture of blue pieces in the mosaic, nor any blue without a little centre of pale green; sometimes only a single piece of glass a quarter of an inch square, so subtle was the feeling for colour which was thus to be satisfied.* The intermediate circles have golden stars set on an azure ground, varied in the same manner; and the small crosses seen in the intervals are alternately blue and subdued scarlet, with two small circles of white set in the golden ground above and beneath them, each only about half an inch across (this work, re- member, being on the outside of the building, and twenty feet above the eye), while the blue crosses have each a pale green centre. Of all this exquisitely mingled hue, no plate, however large or expensive, could give any adequate con- ception; but, if the reader will supply in ima- gination to the engraving what he supplies to a common woodcut of a group of flowers, the decision of the respective merits of modern and

---

* The fact is, that no two tesseræ of the glass are exactly of the same tint, the greens being all varied with blues, the blues of different depths, the reds of different clearness, so that the effect of each mass of colour is full of variety, like the stippled colour of a fruit piece. [Messrs. Salviati have, of course, put all this to rights in the new floor, and made it as flat as an oilcloth long ago—1877.]

of Byzantine architecture may be allowed to rest
on this fragment of St. Mark's alone.

From the vine-leaves of that archivolt, though
there is no direct imitation of nature in them,
but, on the contrary, a studious subjection to
architectural purpose more particularly to be
noticed hereafter, we may yet receive the same
kind of pleasure which we have in seeing true
vine-leaves and wreathed branches traced upon
golden light; its stars upon their azure ground
ought to make us remember, as its builder remembered, the stars that ascend and fall in the
great arch of the sky; and I believe that stars,
and boughs, and leaves, and bright colours are
everlastingly lovely, and to be by all men beloved; and moreover, that church walls grimly
seared with square lines, are not better nor
nobler things than these. I believe the man who
designed and the man who delighted in that
archivolt to have been wise, happy, and holy.
Let the reader look back to the archivolt I have
already given out of the streets of London,* and
see what there is in it to make us any of the
three. Let him remember that the men who
design such work as that call St. Mark's a
barbaric monstrosity, and let him judge between
us.

§ L. Some farther details of the St. Mark's

---

* Rusticated, from a London club-house.

architecture, and also some illustration of the
value of the shafts as large jewels, will be
found in Appendix 9, "Shafts of St. Mark's."
Here I must pass on to the second part of our
immediate subject, namely, the inquiry how far
the exquisite and varied ornament of St. Mark's
fits it, as a temple, for its sacred purpose, and
would be applicable in the churches of modern
times. We have here evidently two questions :
the first, that wide and continually agitated
one, whether richness of ornament be right in
churches at all; the second, whether the ornament of St. Mark's be of a truly ecclesiastical
and Christian character.

§ LI. In the first chapter of the 'Seven Lamps
of Architecture ' I endeavoured to lay before the
reader some reasons why churches ought to be
richly adorned, as being the only places in which
the desire of offering a portion of all precious
things to God could be legitimately expressed.
But I left wholly untouched the question whether
the church, as such, stood in need of adornment,
or would be better fitted for its purposes by
possessing it. This question I would now ask
the reader to deal with briefly and candidly.

The chief difficulty in deciding it has arisen
from its being always presented to us in an un-
fair form. It is asked of us, or we ask of ourselves, whether the sensation which we now feel
in passing from our own modern dwelling-house,

through a newly built street, into a cathedral of the thirteenth century, be safe or desirable as a preparation for public worship. But we never ask whether that sensation was at all calculated upon by the builders of the cathedral.

§ LII. Now I do not say that the contrast of the ancient with the modern building, and the strangeness with which the earliest architectural forms fall upon the eye, are at this day disadvantageous. But I do say, that their effect, whatever it may be, was entirely uncalculated upon by the old builder. He endeavoured to make his work beautiful, but never expected it to be *strange*. And we incapacitate ourselves altogether from fair judgment of its intention, if we forget that, when it was built, it rose in the midst of other work fanciful and beautiful as itself; that every dwelling-house in the middle ages was rich with the same ornaments and quaint with the same grotesques which fretted the porches or animated the gargoyles of the cathedral; that what we now regard with doubt and wonder, as well as with delight, was then the natural continuation, into the principal edifice of the city, of a style which was familiar to every eye throughout all its lanes and streets; and that the architect had often no more idea of producing a peculiarly devotional impression by the richest colour and the most elaborate carving, than the builder of a modern meeting-house has by his whitewashed walls and square-cut casements.*

§ LIII. Let the reader fix this great fact well in his mind, and then follow out its important corollaries. We attach, in modern days, a kind of sacredness to the pointed arch and the groined roof, because, while we look habitually out of square windows and live under flat ceilings, we meet with the more beautiful forms in the ruins of our abbeys. But when those abbeys were built, the pointed arch was used for every shop door, as well as for that of the cloister, and the feudal baron and freebooter feasted, as the monk sang, under vaulted roofs; not because the vaulting was thought especially appropriate to either the revel or psalm, but because it was then the form in which a strong roof was easiest built. We have destroyed the goodly architecture of our cities; we have substituted one wholly devoid of beauty or meaning; and then we reason respecting the strange effect upon our minds of the fragments which, fortunately, we have left in our churches, as if those churches had always been designed to stand out in strong relief from all the buildings around them, and Gothic architecture had always been, what it is now, a religious language, like Monkish Latin. Most readers know, if they would arouse their

* Compare my Oxford lecture, (in the inaugural series,) on the relation of Art to Religion.

knowledge, that this was not so; but they take no pains to reason the matter out: they abandon themselves drowsily to the impression that Gothic is a peculiarly ecclesiastical style; and sometimes, even, that richness in church ornament is a condition or furtherance of the Romish religion. Undoubtedly it has become so in modern times: for there being no beauty in our recent architecture, and much in the remains of the past, and these remains being almost exclusively ecclesiastical, the High Church and Romanist parties have not been slow in availing themselves of the natural instincts which were deprived of all food except from this source; and have willingly promulgated the theory, that because all the good architecture that is now left is expressive of High Church or Romanist doctrines, all good architecture ever has been and must be so,—a piece of absurdity from which, though here and there a country clergyman may innocently believe it, I hope the common sense of the nation will soon manfully quit itself. It needs but little inquiry into the spirit of the past, to ascertain what, once for all, I would desire here clearly and forcibly to assert, that wherever Christian church architecture has been good and lovely, it has been merely the perfect development of the common dwelling-house architecture of the period; that when the pointed arch was used in the street, it was

used in the church; when the round arch was
used in the street, it was used in the church;
when the pinnacle was set over the garret
window, it was set over the belfry tower; when
the flat roof was used for the drawing-room, it
was used for the nave. There is no sacredness
in round arches, nor in pointed; none in pinnacles, nor in buttresses; none in pillars, nor in
traceries. Churches were larger than most other
buildings, because they had to hold more people;
they were more adorned than most other buildings, because they were safer from violence, and
were the fitting subjects of devotional offering:
but they were never built in any separate,
mystical, and religious style; they were built
in the manner that was common and familiar
to everybody at the time. The flamboyant
traceries that adorn the façade of Rouen Cathedral had once their fellows in every window
of every house in the market-place; the sculptures that adorn the porches of St. Mark's had
once their match on the walls of every palace
on the Grand Canal; and the only difference
between the church and the dwelling-house
was, that there existed a symbolical meaning
in the distribution of the parts of all buildings
meant for worship, and that the painting or
sculpture was, in the one case, less frequently
of profane subject than in the other. A more
severe distinction cannot be drawn; for secular

history was constantly introduced into church architecture; and sacred history or allusion generally formed at least one-half of the ornament of the dwelling-house.

§ LIV. This fact is so important, and so little considered, that I must be pardoned for dwelling upon it at some length, and accurately marking the limits of the assertion I have made. I do not mean that every dwelling-house of mediæval cities was as richly adorned and as exquisite in composition as the fronts of their cathedrals, but that they presented features of the same kind, often in parts quite as beautiful; and that the churches were not separated by any change of style from the buildings round them, as they are now, but were merely more finished and full examples of a universal style, rising out of the confused streets of the city as an oak tree does out of an oak copse, not differing in leafage, but in size and symmetry. Of course the quainter and smaller forms of turret and window necessary for domestic service, the inferior materials, often wood instead of stone, and the fancy of the inhabitants, which had free play in the design, introduced oddnesses, vulgarities, and variations into house architecture, which were prevented by the traditions, the wealth, and the skill of the monks and freemasons; while, on the other hand, conditions of vaulting, buttressing, and arch and tower

building, were necessitated by the mere size of
the cathedral, of which it would be difficult to
find examples elsewhere. But there was nothing
more in these features than the adaptation of
mechanical skill to vaster requirements; there
was nothing intended to be, or felt to be,
especially ecclesiastical in any of the forms so
developed; and the inhabitants of every village
and city, when they furnished funds for the
decoration of their church, desired merely to
adorn the house of God as they adorned their
own, only a little more richly, and with a somewhat graver temper in the subjects of the carving. Even this last difference is not always
clearly discernible: all manner of ribaldry occurs
in the details of the ecclesiastical buildings of
the North, and at the time when the best of
them were built, every man's house was a kind
of temple; a figure of the Madonna, or of Christ,
almost always occupied a niche over the principal
door, and the Old Testament histories were
curiously interpolated amidst the grotesques of
the brackets and the gables.

§ LV. And the reader will now perceive that
the question respecting fitness of church decoration rests in reality on totally different grounds
from those commonly made foundations of argument. So long as our streets are walled with
barren brick, and our eyes rest continually, in
our daily life, on objects utterly ugly, or of

inconsistent and meaningless design, it may be a doubtful question whether the faculties of eye and mind which are capable of perceiving beauty, having been left without food during the whole of our active life, should be suddenly feasted upon entering a place of worship; and colour, and music, and sculpture should delight the senses, and stir the curiosity of men unaccustomed to such appeal, at the moment when they are required to compose themselves for acts of devotion;—this, I say, may be a doubtful question: but it cannot be a question at all, that if once familiarized with beautiful form and colour, and accustomed to see in whatever human hands have executed for us, even for the lowest services, evidence of noble thought and admirable skill, we shall desire to see this evidence also in whatever is built or laboured for the house of prayer; that the absence of the accustomed loveliness would disturb instead of assisting devotion; and that we should feel it as vain to ask whether, with our own house full of goodly craftsmanship, we should worship God in a house destitute of it, as to ask whether a pilgrim whose day's journey had led him through fair woods and by sweet waters, must at evening turn aside into some barren place to pray.

§ LVI. Then the second question submitted to us, whether the ornament of St. Mark's be truly ecclesiastical and Christian, is evidently

determined together with the first; for, if not
only the permission of ornament at all, but the
beautiful execution of it, be dependent on our
being familiar with it in daily life, it will follow
that no style of noble architecture *can* be exclusively ecclesiastical. It must be practised in the
dwelling before it be perfected in the church,
and it is the test of a noble style that it shall
be applicable to both ; for if essentially false and
ignoble, it may be made to fit the dwelling-
house, but never can be made to fit the church :
and just as there are many principles which will
bear the light of the world's opinion, yet will
not bear the light of God's word, while all
principles which will bear the test of Scripture
will also bear that of practice, so in architecture
there are many forms which expediency and
convenience may apparently justify, or at least
render endurable, in daily use, which will yet
be found offensive the moment they are used
for church service; but there are none good for
church service which cannot bear daily use.
Thus the Renaissance manner of building is a
convenient style for dwelling-houses, but the
natural sense of all religious men causes them
to turn from it with pain when it has been used
in churches; and this has given rise to the
popular idea that the Roman style is good for
houses and the Gothic for churches. This is not
so ; the Roman style is essentially base, and we

can bear with it only so long as it gives us
convenient windows and spacious rooms; the
moment the question of convenience is set aside,
and the expression or beauty of the style is tried
by its being used in a church, we find it fail.

But because the Gothic and Byzantine styles
are fit for churches, they are not therefore less
fit for dwellings. They are in the highest sense
fit and good for both, nor were they ever
brought to perfection except where they were
used for both.

§ LVII. But there is one character of Byzantine work which, according to the time at which
it was employed, may be considered as either fitting or unfitting it for distinctively ecclesiastical
purposes; I mean the essentially pictorial character of its decorations. We have already seen what
large surfaces it leaves void of bold architectural
features, to be rendered interesting merely by
surface ornament or sculpture. In this respect
Byzantine work differs essentially from pure
Gothic styles, which are capable of filling every
vacant space by features purely architectural,
and may be rendered, if we please, altogether
independent of pictorial aid. A Gothic church
may be rendered impressive by mere successions
of arches, accumulations of niches, and entangle-
ments of tracery. But a Byzantine church requires expression and interesting decoration over
vast plain surfaces,—decoration which becomes

noble only by becoming pictorial; that is to say, by representing natural objects—men, animals, or flowers. And, therefore, the question whether the Byzantine style be fit for church service in modern days, becomes involved in the inquiry what effect upon religion has been or may yet be produced by pictorial art, and especially by the art of the mosaicist?

§ LVIII. The more I have examined this subject, the more dangerous I have found it to dogmatize respecting the character of the art which is likely, at a given period, to be most useful to the cause of religion. One great fact first meets me. I cannot answer for the experience of others, but I never yet met with a Christian whose heart was thoroughly set upon the world to come, and, so far as human judgment could pronounce, perfect and right before God, who cared about art at all. I have known several very noble Christian men who loved it intensely, but in them there was always traceable some entanglement of the thoughts with the matters of this world, causing them to fall into strange distresses and doubts, and often leading them into what they themselves would confess to be errors in understanding, or even failures in duty. I do not say that these men may not, many of them, be in very deed nobler than those whose conduct is more consistent; they may be more tender in the tone of all their feelings, and farther-sighted in soul, and for that very reason exposed to greater trials and fears, than those whose hardier frame and naturally narrower vision enable them with less effort to give their hands to God and walk with Him. But still, the general fact is indeed so, that I have never known a man who seemed altogether right and calm in faith, who seriously cared about art; and when casually moved by it, it is quite impossible to say beforehand by what class of art this impression will on such men be made. Very often it is by a theatrical commonplace, more frequently still by false sentiment. I believe that the four painters who have had, and still have, the most influence, such as it is, on the ordinary Protestant Christian mind, are Carlo Dolci, Guercino, Benjamin West, and John Martin. Raphael, much as he is talked about, is, I believe in very fact, rarely looked at by religious people; much less his master, or any of the truly great religious men of old. But a smooth Magdalen of Carlo Dolci with a tear on each cheek, or a Guercino Christ or St. John, or a Scripture illustration of West's, or a black cloud with a flash of lightning in it of Martin's, rarely fails of being verily, often deeply, felt for the time.

§ LIX. There are indeed many very evident reasons for this; the chief one being that, as all truly great religious painters have been hearty

Romanists, there are none of their works which
do not embody, in some portions of them,
definitely Romanist doctrines. The Protestant
mind is instantly struck by these, and offended
by them, so as to be incapable of entering, or at
least rendered indisposed to enter, farther into
the heart of the work, or to the discovering those
deeper characters of it, which are not Romanist,
but Christian, in the everlasting sense and power ·
of Christianity. Thus most Protestants, entering for the first time a Paradise of Angelico,
would be irrevocably offended by finding that
the first person the painter wished them to
speak to was St. Dominic; and would retire
from such a heaven as speedily as possible,—
not giving themselves time to discover, that
whether dressed in black or white or grey, and
by whatever name in the calendar they might
be called, the figures that filled that Angelico
heaven were indeed more saintly, and pure, and
full of love in every feature, than any that the
human hand ever traced before or since. And
thus Protestantism, having foolishly sought for
the little help it requires at the hand of painting
from the men who embodied no Catholic doctrine,
has been reduced to receive it from those who
believed neither Catholicism nor Protestantism,
but who read the Bible in search of the picturesque. We thus refuse to regard the painters
who passed their lives in prayer, but are perfectly

ready to be taught by those who spent them in
debauchery. There is perhaps no more popular
Protestant picture than Salvator's " Witch of
Endor," of which the subject was chosen by the
painter, simply because, under the names of Saul
and the Sorceress, he could paint a captain of
banditti, and a Neapolitan hag.

§ LX. The fact seems to be that strength of
religious feeling is capable of supplying for itself
whatever is wanting in the rudest suggestions of
art, and will either, on the one hand, purify what
is coarse into inoffensiveness, or, on the other,
raise what is feeble into impressiveness. Probably all art, as such, is unsatisfactory to it; and
the effort which it makes to supply the void will
be induced rather by association and accident
than by the real merit of the work submitted to
it. The likeness to a beloved friend, the corre-
spondence with a habitual conception, the freedom
from any strange or offensive particularity, and,
above all, an interesting choice of incident, will
win admiration for a picture when the noblest
efforts of religious imagination would otherwise
fail of power. How much more, when to the
quick capacity of emotion is joined a childish
trust that the picture does indeed represent a
fact! It matters little whether the fact be well
or ill told: the moment we believe the picture to
be true, we complain little of its being ill-painted.
Let it be considered for a moment, whether the

child, with its coloured print, inquiring eagerly
and gravely which is Joseph, and which is Benjamin, is not more capable of receiving a strong,
even a sublime, impression from the rude symbol
which it invests with reality by its own effort,
than the connoisseur who admires the grouping
of the three figures in Raphael's "Telling of
the Dreams;" and whether also, when the human
mind is in right religious tone, it has not always
this childish power—I speak advisedly, this power
—a noble one, and possessed more in youth
than at any period of after life, but always, I
think, restored in a measure by religion—of
raising into sublimity and reality the rudest
symbol which is given to it of accredited
truth.

§ LXI. Ever since the period of the Renaissance,
however, the truth has not been accredited; the
painter of a religious subject is no longer regarded as the narrator of a fact, but as the inventor
of an idea.* We do not severely criticise the
manner in which a true history is told, but we
become harsh investigators of the faults of an

* I do not mean that modern Christians believe less in the
facts than ancient Christians (I ought to have meant it though,
and very sternly.—*Author's note in* 1879), but they do not
believe in the representation of the facts as true. We look upon
the picture as this or that painter's conception; the elder
Christians looked upon it as this or that painter's description of
what had actually taken place. And in the Greek Church all
painting is, to this day, strictly a branch of tradition. See M.

invention; so that in the modern religious mind,
the capacity of emotion, which renders judgment
uncertain, is joined with an incredulity which
renders it severe; and this ignorant emotion,
joined with ignorant observance of faults, is the
worst possible temper in which any art can be
regarded, but more especially sacred art. For
as religious faith renders emotion facile, so also
it generally renders expression simple; that is to
say, a truly religious painter will very often be
ruder, quainter, simpler, and more faulty in his
manner of working, than a great irreligious one.
And it was in this artless utterance, and simple
acceptance, on the part of both the workman and
the beholder, that all noble schools of art have
been cradled; it is in them that they *must* be
cradled to the end of time. It is impossible to
calculate the enormous loss of power in modern
days, owing to the imperative requirement that
art shall be methodical and learned: for as long
as the constitution of this world remains un-
altered, there will be more intellect in it than
there can be education; there will be many men
capable of just sensation and vivid invention,

Dideron's admirably written introduction to his Iconographie
Chrétienne, p. 7 :—" Un de mes compagnons s'étonnait de
retrouver à la Panagia de St. Luc, le saint Jean Chrysostome
qu'il avait dessiné dans le baptistère de St. Marc, à Venise. Le
costume des personnages est partout et en tout temps le même,
non-seulement pour la forme, mais pour la couleur, mais pour
le dessin, mais jusque pour le nombre et l'épaisseur des plis."

who never will have time to cultivate or polish
their natural powers. And all unpolished power
is in the present state of society lost; in other
things as well as in the arts, but in the arts
especially; nay, in nine cases out of ten, people
mistake the polish for the power. Until a man
has passed through a course of academy studentship, and can draw in an improved manner with
French chalk, and knows foreshortening, and
perspective, and something of anatomy, we do
not think he can possibly be an artist; what is
worse, we are very apt to think that we can
make him an artist by teaching him anatomy,
and how to draw with French chalk; whereas
the real gift in him is utterly independent of all
such accomplishments: and I believe there are
many peasants on every estate, and labourers in
every town, of Europe, who have imaginative
powers of a high order, which nevertheless cannot
be used for our good, because we do not choose
to look at anything but what is expressed in a
legal and scientific way. I believe there is many
a village mason who, set to carve a series of
Scripture or any other histories, would find many
a strange and noble fancy in his head and set it
down, roughly enough indeed, but in a way well
worth our having. But we are too grand to let
him do this, or to set up his clumsy work when
it is done; and accordingly the poor stone-mason
is kept hewing stones smooth at the corners, and

we build our church of the smooth square stones,
and consider ourselves wise.

§ LXII. I shall pursue this subject farther in
another place; but I allude to it here in order
to meet the objections of those persons who suppose the mosaics of St. Mark's, and others of the
period, to be utterly barbarous as representations
of religious history. Let it be granted that they
are so; we are not for that reason to suppose they
were ineffective in religious teaching. I have
above spoken of the whole church as a great Book
of Common Prayer; the mosaics were its illuminations, and the common people of the time
were taught their Scripture history by means of
them, more impressively perhaps, though far less
fully, than ours are now by Scripture reading.
They had no other Bible, and—Protestants do not
often enough consider this—*could* have no other.
We find it somewhat difficult to furnish our poor
with printed Bibles; consider what the difficulty
must have been when they could be given only
in manuscript. The walls of the church necessarily became the poor man's Bible, and a picture was more easily read upon the walls than a
chapter. Under this view, and considering them
merely as the Bible pictures of a great nation in
its youth, I shall finally invite the reader to examine the connexion and subjects of these mosaics;
but in the meantime I have to deprecate the idea
of their execution being in any sense barbarous.

I have conceded too much to modern prejudice, in permitting them to be rated as mere childish efforts at coloured portraiture : they have characters in them of a very noble kind ; nor are they by any means devoid of the remains of the science of the later Roman empire.   The character of the features is almost always fine, the expression stern and quiet, and very solemn, the attitudes and draperies always majestic in the single figures, and in those of the groups which are not in violent action ; * while the bright colouring and disregard of chiaroscuro cannot be regarded as imperfections, since they are the only means by which the figures could be rendered clearly intelligible in the distance and darkness of the vaulting.   So far am I from considering them barbarous, that I believe of all works of religious art whatsoever, these, and such as these, have been the most effective.   They stand exactly midway between the debased manufacture of wooden and waxen images which is the support of Romanist idolatry all over the world, and the

* All the efforts of Byzantine art to represent violent action are inadequate, most of them ludicrously so, even when the sculptural art is in other respects far advanced.   The early Gothic sculptors, on the other hand, fail in all points of refinement, but hardly ever in expression of action.   This distinction is of course one of the necessary consequences of the difference in all respects between the repose of the Eastern, and activity of the Western, mind, which we shall have to trace out completely in the inquiry into the nature of Gothic.

great art which leads the mind away from the religious subject to the art itself. Respecting neither of these branches of human skill is there, nor can there be, any question. The manufacture of puppets, however influential on the Romanist mind of Europe, is certainly not deserving of consideration as one of the fine arts. It matters literally nothing to a Romanist what the image he worships is like. Take the vilest doll that is screwed together in a cheap toy-shop, trust it to the keeping of a large family of children, let it be beaten about the house by them till it is reduced to a shapeless block, then dress it in a satin frock and declare it to have fallen from heaven, and it will satisfactorily answer all Romanist purposes. Idolatry,* it cannot be too often repeated, is no encourager of the fine arts. But, on the other hand, the highest branches of the fine arts are no encouragers either of idolatry or of religion. No picture of Leonardo's or Raphael's, no statue of Michael Angelo's, has ever been worshipped, except by accident. Carelessly regarded, and by ignorant persons, there is less to attract in them than in commoner works. Carefully regarded, and by intelligent persons, they instantly divert the mind from their subject to their art, so that admiration takes the place of devotion. I do not say that the Madonna di S.

* Appendix 10 (old edition): "Proper Sense of the word Idolatry."

Sisto, the Madonna del Cardellino, and such others, have not had considerable religious influence on certain minds, but I say that on the mass of the people of Europe they have had none whatever; while by far the greater number of the most celebrated statues and pictures are never regarded with any other feelings than those of admiration of human beauty, or reverence for human skill. Effective religious art, therefore, has always lain, and I believe must always lie, between the two extremes—of barbarous idol-fashioning on one side, and magnificent craftsmanship on the other. It consists partly in missal-painting, and such book-illustrations as, since the invention of printing, have taken its place; partly in glass-painting; partly in rude sculpture on the outsides of buildings; partly in mosaics; and partly in the frescoes and tempera pictures which, in the fourteenth century, formed the link between this powerful, because imperfect, religious art, and the impotent perfection which succeeded it.

§ LXIII. But of all these branches the most important are the inlaying and mosaic of the twelfth and thirteenth centuries, represented in a central manner by these mosaics of St. Mark's. Missal-painting could not, from its minuteness, produce the same sublime impressions, and frequently merged itself in mere ornamentation of the page. Modern book-illustration has been so little

skilful as hardly to be worth naming. Sculpture, though in some positions it becomes of great
importance, has always a tendency to lose itself in
architectural effect; and was probably seldom deciphered, in all its parts, by the common people,
still less the traditions annealed in the purple
burning of the painted window. Finally, tempera
pictures and frescoes were often of limited size
or of feeble colour. But the great mosaics of
the twelfth and thirteenth centuries covered the
walls and roofs of the churches with inevitable
lustre; they could not be ignored or escaped from;
their size rendered them majestic, their distance
mysterious, their colour attractive. They did
not pass into confused or inferior decorations;
neither were they adorned with any evidences of
skill or science, such as might withdraw the
attention from their subjects. They were before
the eyes of the devotee at every interval of his
worship; vast shadowings forth of scenes to
whose realization he looked forward, or of spirits
whose presence he invoked. And the man must
be little capable of receiving a religious impression of any kind, who, to this day, does not
acknowledge some feeling of awe, as he looks
up to the pale countenances and ghastly forms
which haunt the dark roofs of the Baptisteries
of Parma and Florence, or remains altogether
untouched by the majesty of the colossal images
of apostles, and of Him who sent apostles, that

look down from the darkening gold of the
domes of Venice and Pisa.

§ LXIV. I shall, in a future portion of this
work, endeavour to discover what probabilities
there are of our being able to use this kind of
art in modern churches; but at present it remains
for us to follow out the connexion of the subjects
represented in St. Mark's, so as to fulfil our
immediate object, and form an adequate conception of the feelings of its builders, and of its uses
to those for whom it was built.

Now there is one circumstance to which I
must, in the outset, direct the reader's special
attention, as forming a notable distinction between ancient and modern days. Our eyes are
now familiar and wearied with writing; and if
an inscription is put upon a building, unless it
be large and clear, it is ten to one whether we
ever trouble ourselves to decipher it. But the
old architect was sure of readers. He knew that
every one would be glad to decipher all that he
wrote; that they would rejoice in possessing the
vaulted leaves of his stone manuscript; and that
the more he gave them, the more grateful would
the people be. We must take some pains, therefore, when we enter St. Mark's, to read all that
is inscribed, or we shall not penetrate into the
feeling either of the builder or of his times.

§ LXV. A large atrium or portico is attached
to two sides of the church, a space which was

especially reserved for unbaptised persons and new converts. It was thought right that, before their baptism, these persons should be led to contemplate the great facts of the Old Testament history; the history of the Fall of Man, and of the lives of Patriarchs up to the period of the Covenant by Moses; the order of the subjects in this series being very nearly the same as in many Northern churches, but significantly closing with the Fall of the Manna, in order to mark to the catechumen the insufficiency of the Mosaic covenant for salvation,—"Our fathers did eat manna in the wilderness, and are dead,"—and to turn his thoughts to the true Bread of which that manna was the type.

§ LXVI. Then, when after his baptism he was permitted to enter the church, over its main entrance he saw, on looking back, a mosaic of Christ enthroned, with the Virgin on one side and St. Mark on the other, in attitudes of adoration. Christ is represented as holding a book open upon His knee, on which is written: "I AM THE DOOR; BY ME IF ANY MAN ENTER IN, HE SHALL BE SAVED." On the red marble moulding which surrounds the mosaic is written: "I AM THE GATE OF LIFE; LET THOSE WHO ARE MINE ENTER BY ME." Above, on the red marble fillet which forms the cornice of the west end of the church, is written, with reference to the figure of Christ below: "WHO HE WAS, AND FROM WHOM

HE CAME, AND AT WHAT PRICE HE REDEEMED THEE, AND WHY HE MADE THEE, AND GAVE THEE ALL THINGS, DO THOU CONSIDER."

Now observe, this was not to be seen and read only by the catechumen when he first entered the church; every one who at any time entered was supposed to look back and to read this writing; their daily entrance into the church was thus made a daily memorial of their first entrance into the spiritual Church; and we shall find that the rest of the book which was opened for them upon its walls continually led them in the same manner to regard the visible temple as in every part a type of the invisible Church of God.

§ LXVII. Therefore the mosaic of the first dome, which is over the head of the spectator as soon as he has entered by the great door (that door being the type of baptism), represents the effusion of the Holy Spirit, as the first consequence and seal of the entrance into the Church of God. In the centre of the cupola is the Dove, enthroned in the Greek manner, as the Lamb is enthroned when the Divinity of the Second and Third Persons is to be insisted upon, together with their peculiar offices. From the central symbol of the Holy Spirit twelve streams of fire descend upon the heads of the twelve apostles, who are represented standing around the dome; and below them, between the windows which are pierced in its walls, are represented, by groups of two

figures for each separate people, the various
nations who heard the apostles speak, at Pente-
cost, every man in his own tongue. Finally, on
the vaults, at the four angles, which support the
cupola, are pictured four angels, each bearing a
tablet upon the end of a rod in his hand ; on each
of the tablets of the three first angels, is inscribed
the word "Holy ;" on that of the fourth is written
"Lord ;" and the beginning of the hymn being
thus put into the mouths of the four angels, the
words of it are continued around the border of
the dome, uniting praise to God for the gift of
the Spirit, with welcome to the redeemed soul
received unto His Church:

"HOLY, HOLY, HOLY, LORD GOD OF SABAOTH:
   HEAVEN AND EARTH ARE FULL OF THY GLORY.
   HOSANNA IN THE HIGHEST:
   BLESSED IS HE THAT COMETH IN THE NAME
     OF THE LORD."

And observe in this writing that the convert
is required to regard the outpouring of the Holy
Spirit especially as a work of *sanctification*. It
is the *holiness* of God manifested in the giving
of His Spirit to sanctify those who had become
His children, which the four angels celebrate in
their ceaseless praise; and it is on account of
this holiness that the heaven and earth are said
to be full of His glory.

§ LXVIII. After thus hearing praise rendered

to God by the angels for the salvation of the
newly-entered soul, it was thought fittest that
the worshipper should be led to contemplate, in
the most comprehensive forms possible, the past
evidence and the future hopes of Christianity,
as summed up in the three facts without assurance of which all faith is vain; namely, that
Christ died, that He rose again, and that He
ascended into Heaven, there to prepare a place
for His elect. On the vault between the first and
second cupolas are represented the crucifixion
and resurrection of Christ, with the usual series
of intermediate scenes—the treason of Judas,
the judgment of Pilate, the crowning with
thorns, the descent into Hades, the visit of the
women to the Sepulchre, and the apparition to
Mary Magdalene. The second cupola itself, which
is the central and principal one of the church, is
entirely occupied by the subject of the Ascension.
At the highest point of it Christ is represented
as rising into the blue heaven, borne up by four
angels, and throned upon a rainbow, the type of
reconciliation. Beneath Him, the twelve apostles
are seen upon the Mount of Olives, with the
Madonna, and, in the midst of them, the two
men in white apparel who appeared at the
moment of the Ascension, above whom, as
uttered by them, are inscribed the words, "Ye
men of Galilee, why stand ye gazing up into
heaven? This Christ, the Son of God, as He

is taken from you, shall so come, the arbiter of the earth, trusted to do judgment and justice."

§ LXIX. Beneath the circle of the apostles, between the windows of the cupola, are represented the Christian virtues, as sequent upon the crucifixion of the flesh, and the spiritual ascension together with Christ. (See note at end of this volume.) Beneath them, on the vaults which support the angles of the cupola, are placed the four Evangelists, because on their evidence our assurance of the fact of the Ascension rests; and finally, beneath their feet, as symbols of the sweetness and fulness of the Gospel which they declared, are represented the four rivers of Paradise—Pison, Gihon, Tigris, and Euphrates.

§ LXX. The third cupola, that over the altar, represents the witness of the Old Testament to Christ; showing Him enthroned in its centre, and surrounded by the patriarchs and prophets. But this dome was little seen by the people; * their contemplation was intended to be chiefly drawn to that of the centre of the church, and thus the mind of the worshipper was at once fixed on the main groundwork and hope of Christianity,—"Christ is risen," and "Christ shall come." If he had time to explore the minor lateral chapels and cupolas, he could find in them the whole series of New Testament history, the

---

* It is also of inferior workmanship, and perhaps later than the rest. Vide Lord Lindsay, vol. i. p. 124, note.

events of the life of Christ, and the Apostolic miracles in their order, and finally the scenery of the Book of Revelation: * but if he only entered, as often the common people do to this hour, snatching a few moments before beginning the labour of the day to offer up an ejaculatory prayer, and advanced but from the main entrance as far as the altar screen, all the splendour of the glittering nave and variegated dome, if they smote upon his heart, as they might often, in strange contrast with his reed cabin among the shallows of the lagoon, smote upon it only that they might proclaim the two great messages,— "Christ is risen," and "Christ shall come." Daily, as the white cupolas rose like wreaths of sea-foam in the dawn, while the shadowy campanile and frowning palace were still withdrawn into the night, they rose with the Easter Voice of Triumph,—"Christ is risen;" and daily, as they looked down upon the tumult of the people, deepening and eddying in the wide square that opened from their feet to the sea, they uttered above them the sentence of warning,— "Christ shall come."

§ LXXI. And this thought may surely dispose the reader to look with some change of temper upon the gorgeous building and wild blazonry

* The old mosaics from the Revelation have perished, and have been replaced by miserable work of the seventeenth century.

of that shrine of St. Mark's. He now perceives
that it was in the hearts of the old Venetian
people far more than a place of worship. It was
at once a type of the Redeemed Church of God,
and a scroll for the written word of God. It
was to be to them, both an image of the Bride,
all glorious within, her clothing of wrought gold;
and the actual Table of the Law and the Testimony, written within and without. And whether
honoured as the Church or as the Bible, was it
not fitting that neither the gold nor the crystal
should be spared in the adornment of it; that, as
the symbol of the Bride, the building of the wall
thereof should be of jasper,* and the foundations
of it garnished with all manner of precious stones;
and that, as the channel of the Word, that
triumphant utterance of the Psalmist should be
true of it,—" I have rejoiced in the way of Thy
testimonies, as much as in all riches "? And
shall we not look with changed temper down
the long perspective of St. Mark's Place towards
the sevenfold gates and glowing domes of its
temple, when we know with what solemn
purpose the shafts of it were lifted above the
pavement of the populous square? Men met
there from all countries of the earth, for traffic
or for pleasure; but, above the crowd swaying
for ever to and fro in the restlessness of avarice
or thirst of delight, was seen perpetually the

* Rev. xxi. 18.

glory of the temple, attesting to them, whether
they would hear or whether they would forbear,
that there was one treasure which the merchant-
man might buy without a price, and one delight
better than all others, in the word and the
statutes of God. Not in the wantonness of
wealth, not in vain ministry to the desire of
the eyes or the pride of life, were those marbles
hewn into transparent strength, and those arches
arrayed in the colours of the iris. There is a
message written in the dyes of them, that once
was written in blood ; and a sound in the echoes
of their vaults, that one day shall fill the vault
of heaven,—"He shall return to do judgment
and justice." The strength of Venice was given
her, so long as she remembered this : her destruction found her when she had forgotten this ;
and it found her irrevocably because she for-
got it without excuse. Never had city a more
glorious Bible. Among the nations of the North,
a rude and shadowy sculpture filled their temples
with confused and hardly legible imagery ; but,
for her, the skill and the treasures of the East
had gilded every letter, and illumined every page,
till the Book-Temple shone from afar off like the
star of the Magi. In other cities, the meetings
of the people were often in places withdrawn
from religious association, subject to violence and
to change ; and on the grass of the dangerous
rampart, and in the dust of the troubled street,

there were deeds done and counsels taken, which,
if we cannot justify, we may sometimes forgive.
But the sins of Venice, whether in her palace or
in her piazza, were done with the Bible at her
right hand. The walls on which its testimony
was written were separated but by a few inches
of marble from those which guarded the secrets
of her councils, or confined the victims of her
policy. And when in her last hours she threw
off all shame and all restraint, and the great
square of the city became filled with the madness of the whole earth, be it remembered how
much her sin was greater, because it was done in
the face of the House of God, burning with the
letters of His Law. Mountebank and masquer
laughed their laugh and went their way; and a
silence has followed them, not unforetold; for
amidst them all, through century after century
of gathering vanity and festering guilt, that
white dome of St. Mark's had uttered in the
dead ear of Venice, "Know thou, that for all
these things God will bring thee into judgment."

CHAPTER V.

THE DUCAL PALACE.

§ I. It was stated in the commencement of the preceding chapter that the Gothic art of Venice was separated by the building of the Ducal Palace into two distinct periods; and that in all the domestic edifices which were raised for half a century after its completion, their characteristic and chiefly effective portions were more or less directly copied from it. The fact is, that the Ducal Palace was the great work of Venice at this period, itself the principal effort of her imagination, employing her best architects in its masonry, and her best painters in its decoration, for a long series of years; and we must receive it as a remarkable testimony to the influence which it possessed over the minds of those who saw it in its progress, that, while in the other cities of Italy every palace and church was rising in some original and daily more daring form, the majesty of this single building was able to give pause to the Gothic imagination in its full career; stayed the restlessness of innovation in an instant, and forbade the powers which had created it thenceforth to exert themselves in new directions, or endeavour to summon an image more attractive.

§ II. The reader will hardly believe that while the architectural invention of the Venetians was thus lost, Narcissus-like, in self-contemplation, the various accounts of the progress of the building thus admired and beloved are so confused as frequently to leave it doubtful to what portion of the palace they refer; and that there is actually, at the time being, a dispute between the best Venetian antiquaries, whether the main façade of the palace be of the fourteenth or fifteenth century. The determination of this question is of course necessary before we proceed. to draw any conclusion from the style of the work; and it cannot be determined without a careful review of the entire history of the palace, and of all the documents relating to it. I trust that this review may not be found tedious,—assuredly it will not be fruitless, bringing many facts before us singularly illustrative of the Venetian character.

§ III. Before, however, the reader can enter upon any enquiry into the history of this building, it is necessary that he should be thoroughly familiar with the arrangement and names of its principal parts, as it at present stands; otherwise he cannot comprehend so much as a single sentence of any of the documents referring to it.

I must do what I can, by the help of a rough plan and bird's-eye view, to give him the necessary topographical knowledge:

Opposite is a rude ground-plan of the buildings round St. Mark's Place: and the following references will clearly explain their relative positions:

A. St. Mark's Place.
B. Piazzetta.
P. V. Procuratie Vecchie.
P. N. (opposite) Procuratie Nuove.
P. L. Libreria Vecchia.
1. Piazzetta de' Leoni.
T. Tower of St. Mark.
F F. Great Façade of St. Mark's Church.
M. St. Mark's. (It is so united with the Ducal Palace, that the separation cannot be indicated in the plan, unless all the walls had been marked, which would have confused the whole.)
D D D. Ducal Palace.
C. Court of Ducal Palace.
c. Porta della Carta.
p. p. Ponte della Paglia (Bridge of Straw).
S. Ponte de' Sospiri (Bridge of Sighs).
R R. Riva de' Schiavoni.
g s. Giant's Stair.
J. Judgment angle.
a. Fig tree angle.

The reader will observe that the Ducal Palace is arranged somewhat in the form of a hollow square, of which one side faces the Piazzetta, B, and another the quay called Riva de' Schiavoni, R R; the third is on the dark canal called the

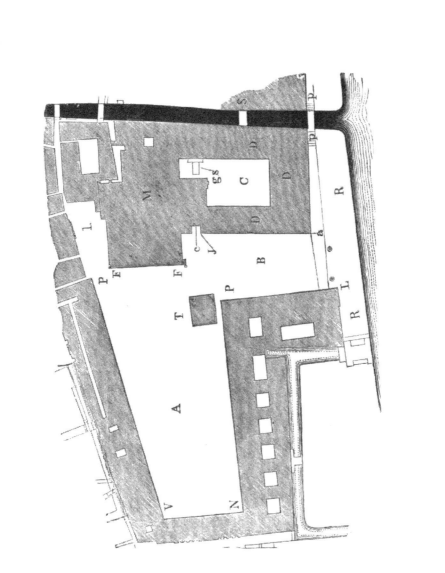

Fig. II. The Ducal Palace—Bird's-eye View.

" Rio del Palazzo," and the fourth joins the
Church of St. Mark.

Of this fourth side, therefore, nothing can be
seen. Of the other three sides we shall have to
speak constantly; and they will be respectively
called, that towards the Piazzetta, the " Piazzetta
Façade ; " that towards the Riva de' Schiavoni,
the " Sea Façade ; " and that towards the Rio del
Palazzo, the " Rio Façade." This Rio, or canal,
is usually looked upon by the traveller with
great respect, or even horror, because it passes
under the Bridge of Sighs. It is, however, one
of the principal thoroughfares of the city ; and
the bridge and its canal together occupy, in the
mind of a Venetian, very much the position of
Fleet Street and Temple Bar in that of a
Londoner,—at least, at the time when Temple
Bar was occasionally decorated with human
heads. The two buildings closely resemble each
other in form.

§ IV. We must now proceed to obtain some
rough idea of the appearance and distribution of
the palace itself; but its arrangement will be
better understood by supposing ourselves raised
some hundred and fifty feet above the point in
the lagoon in front of it, so as to get a general
view of the Sea Façade and Rio Façade (the
latter in very steep perspective), and to look
down into its interior court. Fig. II. roughly
represents such a view, omitting all details on

the roofs, in order to avoid confusion. In this
drawing we have merely to notice that, of the
two bridges seen on the right, the uppermost,
above the black canal, is the Bridge of Sighs;
the lower one is the Ponte della Paglia, the
regular thoroughfare from quay to quay, and, I
believe, called the Bridge of Straws, because the
boats which brought straw from the mainland
used to sell it at this place. The corner of the
palace, rising above this bridge, and formed by
the meeting of the Sea Façade and Rio Façade,
will always be called the Vine angle, because it
is decorated by a sculpture of the drunkenness
of Noah. The angle opposite will be called
the Fig-tree angle, because it is decorated by
a sculpture of the Fall of Man. The long and
narrow range of building, of which the roof is
seen in perspective behind this angle, is the part
of the palace fronting the Piazzetta; and the
angle under the pinnacle most to the left of
the two which terminate it will be called, for
a reason presently to be stated, the Judgment
angle. Within the square formed by the building is seen its interior court (with one of its
wells), terminated by small and fantastic buildings of the Renaissance period, which face the
Giant's Stair, of which the extremity is seen
sloping down on the left.

§ v. The great façade which fronts the
spectator looks southward. Hence the two

traceried windows lower than the rest, and to
the right of the spectator, may be conveniently
distinguished as the "Eastern Windows." There
are two others like them, filled with tracery, and
at the same level, which look upon the narrow
canal between the Ponte della Paglia and the
Bridge of Sighs : these we may conveniently call
the "Canal Windows." The reader will observe
a vertical line in this dark side of the palace,
separating its nearer and plainer wall from a
long four-storied range of rich architecture.
This more distant range is entirely Renaissance :
its extremity is not indicated, because I have no
accurate sketch of the small buildings and bridges
beyond it, and we shall have nothing whatever
to do with this part of the palace in our present inquiry. The nearer and undecorated
wall is part of the older
palace, though much defaced
by modern opening of com-
mon windows, refittings of the
brickwork, etc.

Fig. III.

§ VI. It will be observed
that the façade is composed
of a smooth mass of wall,
sustained on two tiers of pillars, one above the
other. The manner in which these support
the whole fabric will be understood at once
by the rough section, Fig. III., which is
supposed to be taken right through the palace

to the interior court, from near the middle
of the Sea Façade. Here *a* and *d* are the
rows of shafts, both in the inner court and on
the façade, which carry the main walls; *b, c* are
solid walls variously strengthened with pilasters.
A, B, C are the three stories of the interior of
the palace.

The reader sees that it is impossible for any
plan to be more simple, and that if the inner
floors and walls of the stories A, B were removed,
there would be left merely the form of a basilica,
—two high walls, carried on ranges of shafts, and
roofed by a low gable.

The stories A, B are entirely modernised, and
divided into confused ranges of small apartments,
among which what vestiges remain of ancient
masonry are entirely undecipherable, except by
investigations such as I have had neither the
time nor, as in most cases they would involve
the removal of modern plastering, the oppor-
tunity, to make.   With the subdivisions of this
story, therefore, I shall not trouble the reader;
but those of the great upper story, C, are highly
important.

§ VII. In the bird's-eye view above Fig. II.,
it will be noticed that the two windows on
the right are lower than the other four of the
façade. In this arrangement there is one of
the most remarkable instances I know of the
daring sacrifice of symmetry to convenience

which was noticed in Chapter VII. as one of the chief noblenesses of the Gothic schools.

The part of the palace in which the two lower windows occur, we shall find, was first built, and arranged in four stories, in order to obtain the necessary number of apartments. Owing to circumstances, of which we shall presently give an account, it became necessary, in the beginning of the fourteenth century, to provide another large and magnificent chamber for the meeting of the Senate. That chamber was added at the side of the older building : but, as only one room was wanted, there was no need to divide the added portion into two stories. The entire height was given to the single chamber, being indeed not too great for just harmony with its enormous length and breadth. And then came the question how to place the windows, whether on a line with the two others, or above them.

The ceiling of the new room was to be adorned by the paintings of the best masters in Venice, and it became of great importance to raise the light near that gorgeous roof, as well as to keep the tone of illumination in the Council Chamber serene; and therefore to introduce light rather in simple masses than in many broken streams. A modern architect, terrified at the idea of violating external symmetry, would have sacrificed both the pictures and the peace of the Council. He would have placed the larger

windows at the same level with the other two,
and have introduced above them smaller windows,
like those of the upper story in the older building, as if that upper story had been continued
along the façade. But the old Venetian thought
of the honour of the paintings, and the comfort
of the Senate, before his own reputation. He
unhesitatingly raised the large windows to their
proper position with reference to the interior of
the chamber, and suffered the external appearance to take care of itself. And I believe the
whole pile rather gains than loses in effect by
the variation thus obtained in the spaces of wall
above and below the windows.

§ VIII. On the party wall, between the second
and third windows, which faces the eastern
extremity of the Great Council Chamber, is
painted the Paradise of Tintoret; and this wall
will therefore be hereafter called the "Wall of
the Paradise."

In nearly the centre of the Sea Façade, and
between the first and second windows of the
Great Council Chamber, is a large window to the
ground, opening on a balcony, which is one of the
chief ornaments of the palace, and will be called
in future the "Sea Balcony."

The façade which looks on the Piazzetta is very
nearly like this to the Sea, but the greater part
of it was built in the fifteenth century, when
people had become studious of their symmetries.

Its side windows are all on the same level. Two light the west end of the Great Council Chamber, one lights a small room anciently called the Quarantia Civil Nuova; the other three, and the central one, with a balcony like that to the sea, light another large chamber, called Sala del Scrutino, or "Hall of Inquiry," which extends to the extremity of the palace above the Porta della Carta.

§ IX. The reader is now well enough acquainted with the topography of the existing building, to be able to follow the accounts of its history.

We have seen above, that there were three principal styles of Venetian architecture: Byzantine, Gothic, and Renaissance.

The Ducal Palace, which was the great work of Venice, was built successively in the three styles. There was a Byzantine Ducal Palace, a Gothic Ducal Palace, and a Renaissance Ducal Palace. The second superseded the first totally: a few stones of it (if indeed so much) are all that is left. But the third superseded the second in part only, and the existing building is formed by the union of the two.

We shall review the history of each in succession.*

* The reader will find it convenient to note the following editions of the printed books which have been principally consulted in the following inquiry. The numbers of the

1st. The BYZANTINE PALACE.

In the year of the death of Charlemagne (813),* the Venetians determined to make the island of Rialto the seat of the government and capital of their state. Their Doge, Angelo or Agnello Participazio, instantly took vigorous means for the enlargement of the small group of buildings which were to be the nucleus of the future Venice. He appointed persons to superintend the raising of the banks of sand, so as to form more secure foundations, and to build wooden bridges over the canals. For the offices of religion, he built the church of St. Mark ; and on, or near, the spot where the Ducal Palace now stands, he built a palace for the administration of the government.†

manuscripts referred to in the Marcian Library are given with the quotations.

    Sansovino. Venetia Descritta. 4to, Venice, 1663.

    Sansovino. Lettera intorno al Palazzo Ducale. 8vo, Venice, 1829.

    Temanza. Antica Pianta di Venezia, with text. Venice, 1780.

    Cadorin. Pareri di XV. Architetti. 8vo, Venice, 1838.

    Filiasi. Memorie storiche. 8vo, Padua, 1811.

    Bettio. Lettera discorsiva del Palazzo Ducale. 8vo, Venice, 1837.

    Selvatico. Architettura di Vegezia. 8vo, Venice, 1847.

  * The year commonly given is 810, as in the Savina Chronicle (Cod. Marcianus) p. 13. " Dell 810 fece principiar el pallazzo Ducal nel luogo ditto Bruolo in confin di S. Moisè, et fece riedificar la isola di Eraclia." The Sagornin Chronicle gives 804 ; and Filiasi, vol. vi. chap. 1, corrects this date to 813.

  † " Amplò la città fornilla di casamenti, e per il culto

The history of the Ducal Palace, therefore, begins with the birth of Venice, and to what remains of it, at this day, is entrusted the last representation of her power.

§ x. Of the exact position and form of this palace of Participazio little is ascertained. Sansovino says that it was "built near the Ponte della Paglia, and answeringly on the Grand Canal," * towards San Giorgio; that is to say, in the place now occupied by the Sea Façade; but

---

d' Iddio e l' amministrazione della guistizia eresse la cappella di S. Marco, e il palazzo di sua residenza."—Pareri, p. 120. Observe, that piety towards God, and justice towards man, have been at least the nominal purposes of every act and institution of ancient Venice. Compare also Temanza, p. 24. " Quello che abbiamo di certo si è che il suddetto Agnello lo cominciò da fondamenti, e così pure la cappella ducale di, S. Marco."

* What I call the Sea, was called " the Grand Canal " by the Venetians, as well as the great water street of the city ; but I prefer calling it " the Sea," in order to distinguish between that street and the broad water in front of the Ducal Palace which, interrupted only by the island of San Giorgio, stretches for many miles to the south, and for more than two to the boundary of the Lido. It was the deeper channel, just in front of the Ducal Palace, continuing the line of the great water street itself, which the Venetians spoke of as " the Grand Canal." The words of Sansovino are ; " Fu cominciato dove si vede, vicino al ponte della paglia, et rispondente sul canal grande." Filiasi says simply : " The palace was built where it now is." " Il palazio fu fatto dove ora pure esiste."—Vol. iii. chap. 27. The Savina Chronicle, already quoted, says : " In the palace called the Bruolo (or Broglio), that is to say, on the Piazzetta."

this was merely the popular report of his day.
We know, however, positively, that it was somewhere upon the site of the existing palace ; and
that it had an important front towards the
Piazzetta, with which, as we shall see hereafter,
the present palace at one period was incorporated.
We know, also, that it was a pile of some magnificence, from the account given by Sagornino of
the visit paid by the Emperor Otho the Great to
the Doge Pietro Orseolo II.   The chronicler says
that the emperor " beheld carefully all the beauty
of the palace ; " * and the Venetian historians express pride in the building's being worthy of an
emperor's examination.   This was after the palace
had been much injured by fire in the revolt
against Candiano IV.† and just repaired, and

---

* " Omni decoritate illius perlustrata."—Sagornino, quoted
by Cadorin and Temanza.

† There is an interesting account of this revolt in Monaci,
p. 68.   Some historians speak of the palace as having been
destroyed entirely ; but that it did not even need important
restorations, appears from Sagornino's expression, quoted by
Cadorin and Temanza.   Speaking of the Doge Participazio, he
says : " Qui Palatii hucusque manentis fuerit fabricator."   The
reparations of the palace are usually attributed to the successor
of Candiano, Pietro Orseolo I. ; but the legend, under the
picture of that Doge in the Council Chamber, speaks only of
his rebuilding St. Mark's and " performing many miracles."
His whole mind seems to have been occupied with ecclesiastical affairs ; and his piety was finally manifested in a way
somewhat startling to the state, by his absconding with a
French priest to St. Michael's, in Gascony, and there becoming
a monk.   What repairs, therefore, were necessary to the Ducal

richly adorned by Orseolo himself, who is spoken
of by Sagornino as having also "adorned the
chapel of the Ducal Palace" (St. Mark's) with
ornaments of marble and gold.* There can be
no doubt whatever that the palace at this period
resembled and impressed the other Byzantine
edifices of the city, such as the Fondaco de' Turchi,
etc., whose remains have been already described;
and that, like them, it was covered with sculpture, and richly adorned with gold and colour.

§ xi. In the year 1106, it was for the second
time injured by fire, † but repaired before 1116,
when it received another emperor, Henry V. (of
Germany), and was again honoured by imperial
praise.‡ Between 1173 and the close of the century, it seems to have been again repaired and
much enlarged by the Doge Sebastian Ziani.
Sansovino says that this Doge not only repaired
it, but "enlarged it in every direction;" § and,

Palace, were left to be undertaken by his son, Orseolo II.,
above named.

* "Quam non modo marmoreo, verum aureo compsit orna-
mento."—*Temanza*, p. 25.

† "L'anno 1106, uscito fuoco d' una casa privata, arse parte
del palazzo."—*Sansovino*. Of the beneficial effect of these
fires, vide Cadorin, pp. 121, 123.

‡ "Urbis situm, ædificiorum decorem, et regiminis æquitatem
multipliciter commendavit."—*Cronaca Dandolo*, quoted by
Cadorin.

§ "Non solamente rinovò il palazzo, ma lo aggrandì per ogni
verso."—*Sansovino*. Zanotta quotes the Altinat Chronicle for
account of these repairs,

after this enlargement, the palace seems to have remained untouched for a hundred years, until, in the commencement of the fourteenth century, the works of the Gothic Palace were begun. As, therefore, the old Byzantine building was, at the time when those works first interfered with it, in the form given to it by Ziani, I shall hereafter always speak of it as the *Ziani* Palace ; and this the rather, because the only chronicler whose words are perfectly clear respecting the existence of part of this palace so late as the year 1422, speaks of it as built by Ziani. The old " Palace, of which half remains to this day, was built, as we now see it, by Sebastian Ziani." *

So far, then, of the Byzantine Palace.

§ XII. 2nd. The GOTHIC PALACE. The reader doubtless recollects that the important change in the Venetian government which gave stability to the aristocratic power took place about the year 1297,† under the Doge Pietro Gradenigo, a man thus characterised by Sansovino :—" A prompt and prudent man, of unconquerable determination and great eloquence, who laid, so to speak, the foundations of the eternity of this republic, by

---

* "El palazzo che anco di mezzo se vede vecchio, per M. Sebastian Ziani fu fatto compir, come el se vede."—*Chronicle of Pietro Dolfino*, Cod. Ven. p. 47. This Chronicle is spoken of by Sansovino as "molto particolare e distinta."—*Sansovino, Venezia descritta*, p. 593.—It terminates in the year 1422.

† See Vol. I., Appendix 3 (old edition).

the admirable regulations which he introduced into the government."

We may now, with some reason, doubt of their admirableness; but their importance, and the vigorous will and intellect of the Doge, are not to be disputed. Venice was in the zenith of her strength, and the heroism of her citizens was displaying itself in every quarter of the world.[*] The acquiescence in the secure establishment of the aristocratic power was an expression, by the people, of respect for the families which had been chiefly instrumental in raising the commonwealth to such a height of prosperity.

The Serrar del Consiglio fixed the numbers of the senate within certain limits, and it conferred upon them a dignity greater than they had ever before possessed. It was natural that the alteration in the character of the assembly should be attended by some change in the size, arrangement, or decoration of the chamber in which they sat.

We accordingly find it recorded by Sansovino, that "in 1301 another saloon was begun on the Rio del Palazzo, *under the Doge Gradenigo,* and finished in 1309, *in which year the Grand Council first sat in it.*"[†] In the first year, therefore, of the fourteenth century, the Gothic Ducal Palace of Venice was begun; and as the

---

* Vide Sansovino's enumeration of those who flourished in the reign of Gradenigo, p. 564.

† Sansovino, 324, 1.

Byzantine Palace was, in its foundation, coeval
with that of the state, so the Gothic Palace was,
in its foundation, coeval with that of the aristocratic power. Considered as the principal representation of the Venetian school of architecture,
the Ducal Palace is the Parthenon of Venice,
and Gradenigo its Pericles.

§ XIII. Sansovino, with a caution very
frequent among Venetian historians, when
alluding to events connected with the Serrar
del Consiglio, does not specially mention the
cause for the requirement of the new chamber;
but the Sivos Chronicle is a little more distinct
in expression. "In 1301, it was determined to
build a great saloon *for the assembling* of the
Great Council, and the room was built which is
now called the Sala del Scrutinio."* *Now*, that
is to say, at the time when the Sivos Chronicle
was written; the room has long ago been

---

* " 1301 fu presa parte di fare una sala grande per la
riduzione del gran consiglio, e fu fatta quella che ora si
chiama dello Scrutinio."—*Cronaca Siros*, quoted by Cadorin.
There is another most interesting entry in the Chronicle of
Magno, relating to this event ; but the passage is so ill written
that I am not sure if I have deciphered it correctly :—" Del
1301 fu preso de fabrichar la sala fo ruina e fu fata (fatta)
quella se adoperava a far el pregadi e fu adopera per far el
Gran Consegio fin 1423, che fu anni 122." This last sentence,
which is of great importance, is luckily unmistakable :—" The
room was used for the meetings of the Great Council until
1423, that is to say, for 122 years."—*Cod. Ven.*, tom. i. p. 126.
The Chronicle extends from 1253 to 1454.

destroyed, and its name given to another
chamber on the opposite side of the palace :
but I wish the reader to remember the date
1301, as marking .the commencement of a great
architectural epoch, in which took place the
first appliance of the energy of the aristocratic
power, and of the Gothic style, to the works of
the Ducal Palace. The operations then begun
were continued, with hardly an interruption,
during the whole period of the prosperity of
Venice. We shall see the new buildings con-
sume, and take the place of, the Ziani Palace,
piece by piece; and when the Ziani Palace was
destroyed, they fed upon themselves; being continued round the square, until, in the sixteenth
century, they reached the point where they had
been begun in the fourteenth, and pursued the
track they had then followed some distance
beyond the junction ; destroying or hiding their
own commencement, as the serpent, which is the
type of eternity, conceals its tail in its jaws.

§ XIV. We cannot, therefore, *see* the extremity
wherein lay the sting and force of the whole
creature,—the chamber, namely, built by the
Doge Gradenigo; but the reader must keep
that commencement and the date of it carefully
in his mind. The body of the Palace Serpent
will soon become visible to us.

The Gradenigo Chamber was somewhere on
the Rio Façade, behind the present position of

the Bridge of Sighs ; *i.e.*, about the point marked
on the roof by the dotted lines in the woodcut ;
it is not known whether low or high, but probably on a first story. The great façade of the
Ziani Palace being, as above mentioned, on the
Piazzetta, this chamber was as far back and out
of the way as possible; secrecy and security
being obviously the points first considered.

§ xv. But the newly constituted Senate had
need of other additions to the ancient palace besides the Council Chamber. A short, but most
significant, sentence is added to Sansovino's account of the construction of that room. " There
were, *near it*," he says, " the Cancellaria, and the
Gheba or *Gabbia*, afterwards called the Little
Tower." *

Gabbia means a " cage ; " and there can be no
question that certain apartments were at this
time added at the top of the palace and on the
Rio Façade, which were to be used as prisons.
Whether any portion of the old Torresella still
remains is a doubtful question ; but the apartments at the top of the palace, in its fourth
story, were still used for prisons as late as the
beginning of the seventeenth century.†   I wish

* " Vi era appresso la Cancellaria, e la Gheba o Gabbia,
chiamata poi Torresella."— P. 324. A small square tower
is seen above the Vine angle in the view of Venice dated
1500, and attributed to Albert Durer. It appears about 25
feet square, and is very probably the Torresella in question.

† Vide Bettio, Lettera, p. 23.

the reader especially to notice that a separate
tower or range of apartments was built for this
purpose, in order to clear the government of the
accusations so constantly made against them, by
ignorant or partial historians, of wanton cruelty
to prisoners. The stories commonly told respecting the "piombi" of the Ducal Palace are utterly
false. Instead of being, as usually reported,
small furnaces under the leads of the palace,
they were comfortable rooms, with good flat
roofs of larch, and carefully ventilated.* The
new chamber, then, and the prisons, being built,
the Great Council first sat in their retired
chamber on the Rio in the year 1309.

§ XVI. Now, observe the significant progress
of events. They had no sooner thus established
themselves in power, than they were disturbed
by the conspiracy of the Tiepolos, in the year
1310. In consequence of that conspiracy the
Council of Ten was created, still under the Doge
Gradenigo; who, having finished his work and
left the aristocracy of Venice armed with this
terrible power, died in the year 1312, some say
by poison. He was succeeded by the Doge
Marino Giorgio, who reigned only one year; and

---

* Bettio, Lettera, p. 20. "Those who wrote without having
seen them described them as covered with lead; and those
who have seen them know that, between their flat timber
roofs and the sloping leaden roof of the palace, the interval is five metres where it is least, and nine where it is
greatest."

then followed the prosperous government of
John Soranzo. There is no mention of any
additions to the Ducal Palace during his reign,
but he was succeeded by that Francesco Dandolo,
the sculptures on whose tomb, still existing in
the cloisters of the Salute, may be compared by
any traveller with those of the Ducal Palace.
Of him it is recorded in the Savina Chronicle:
"This Doge also had the great gate built which
is at the entry of the palace, above which is his
statue kneeling, with the gonfalon in hand, before the feet of the Lion of St. Mark's." *

§ XVII. It appears, then, that after the Senate
had completed their Council Chamber and the
prisons, they required a nobler door than that
of the old Ziani Palace for their Magnificences
to enter by. This door is twice spoken of in
the government accounts of expenses, which are
fortunately preserved,† in the following terms :—

"1335, June 1.   We, Andrew Dandolo and Mark
       Loredano, procurators of St. Mark's, have
       paid to Martin the stonecutter and his
       associates ‡.   .   .   , for a stone of which

* "Questo Dose anche fese far la porta granda che se al
intrar del Palazzo, in su la qual vi e la sua statua che sta
in zenocchioni con lo confalon in man, davanti li pie de lo
Lion S. Marco."—*Savin Chronicle*, Cod. Ven. p. 120.

† These documents I have not examined myself, being
satisfied of the accuracy of Cadorin, from whom I take the
passages quoted.

‡ "Libras tres, soldos 15 grossorum."—*Cadorin*, 189, 1.

the lion is made which is put over the gate of the palace."

" 1344, November 4. We have paid thirty-five golden ducats for making gold leaf, to gild the lion which is over the door of the palace stairs."

The position of this door is disputed, and is of no consequence to the reader, the door itself having long ago disappeared, and been replaced by the Porta della Carta.

§ XVIII. But before it was finished, occasion had been discovered for further improvements. The Senate found their new Council Chamber inconveniently small, and, about thirty years after its completion, began to consider where a larger and more magnificent one might be built. The government was now thoroughly established, and it was probably felt that there was some meanness in the retired position, as well as in-sufficiency in the size, of the Council Chamber on the Rio. The first definite account which I find of their proceedings, under these circum-stances, is in the Caroldo Chronicle : *

" 1340. On the 28th of December, in the preceding year, Master Marco Erizzo, Nicolo Soranzo, and Thomas Gradenigo, were chosen to examine where a new saloon might be built, in order to assemble therein the Greater Council. . . . . On the 3rd of June, 1341, the Great

* Cod. Ven., No. CXLI. p. 365.

Council elected two procurators of the work of
this saloon, with a salary of eighty ducats a
year."

. It appears from the entry still preserved in
the Archivio, and quoted by Cadorin, that it was
on the 28th of December, 1340, that the com-
missioners appointed to decide on this important
matter gave in their report to the Grand Council,
and that the decree passed thereupon for the
commencement of a new Council Chamber on
the Grand Canal.*

*The room then begun is the one now in exist-
ence,* and its building involved the building of
all that is best and most beautiful in the present
Ducal palace, the rich arcades of the lower stories
being all prepared for sustaining this Sala del
Gran Consiglio.

§ XIX. In saying that it is the same now in
existence, I do not mean that it has undergone
no alterations: as we shall see hereafter, it has
been refitted again and again, and some portions
of its walls rebuilt; but in the place and form in
which it first stood, it still stands; and by a
glance at the position which its windows occupy,
as shown in Fig. II. above, the reader will see at

* Sansovino is more explicit than usual in his reference
to this decree : " For it having appeared that the place (the
first Council Chamber) was not capacious enough, the saloon
on the Grand Canal was ordered." " Per cio parendo che il
luogo non fosse capace, fu ordinata la Sala sul Canal Grande."
—P. 324.

once that whatever can be known respecting the design of the Sea Façade, must be gleaned out of the entries which refer to the building of this Great Council Chamber.

Cadorin quotes two of great importance, to which we shall return in due time, made during the progress of the work in 1342 and 1344 ; then one of 1349, resolving that the works at the Ducal Palace, which had been discontinued during the plague, should be resumed ; and finally one in 1362, which speaks of the Great Council Chamber as having been neglected and suffered to fall into "great desolation," and resolves that it shall be forthwith completed.*

The interruption had not been caused by the plague only, but by the conspiracy of Faliero, and the violent death of the master builder.† The work was resumed in 1362, and completed within the next three years, at least so far as that Guariento was enabled to paint his Paradise on the walls ;‡ so that the building must, at any rate, have been roofed by this time. Its decorations and fittings, however, were long in completion ; the paintings on the roof being only

* Cadorin, 185, 2. The decree of 1342 is falsely given as of 1345 by the Sivos Chronicle, and by Magno ; while Sanuto gives the decree to its right year, 1342, but speaks of the Council Chamber as only begun in 1345.

† Calendario. See Appendix 1, Vol. III. (old edition).

‡ "Il primo che vi colorisse fu Guariento, il quale l' anno 1365 vi fece il Paradiso in testa dellasala."—*Sansovino.*

executed in 1400.*   They represented the heavens
covered with stars, † this being, says Sansovino,
the bearings of the Doge Steno. Almost all
ceilings and vaults were at this time in Venice
covered with stars, without any reference to
armorial bearings; but Steno claims, under his
noble title of Stellifer, an important share in
completing the chamber, in an inscription upon
two square tablets, now inlaid in the walls on
each side of the great window towards the sea:

"MILLE QUADRINGENTI CURREBANT QUATUOR ANNI
    HOC OPUS ILLUSTRIS MICHAEL DUX STELLIFER AUXIT."

And in fact it is to this Doge that we owe the
beautiful balcony of that window, though the
work above it is partly of more recent date;
and I think the tablets bearing this important
inscription have been taken out and reinserted
in the newer masonry. The labour of these
final decorations occupied a total period of sixty
years.

The Grand Council sat in the finished chamber
for the first time in 1423. In that year the

---

* "L' an poi 1400 vi fece il cielo compartita a quadretti
d' oro, ripieni di stelle, ch' era la insegna del Doge Steno."—
Sansovino, lib. VIII.

† "In questi tempi si messe in oro il cielo della sala del
Gran Consiglio et si fece il pergolo del finestra grande che
guarda sul canale, adornato l' uno e l' altro di stelle, ch' erano
l' insegne del Doge."—*Sansovino*, lib. XIII. Compare also
Pareri, p. 129,

Gothic Ducal Palace of Venice was completed. It had taken, to build it, the energies of the entire period which I have above described as the central one of her life.

§ XX. 3rd. The RENAISSANCE PALACE. I must go back a step or two, in order to be certain that the reader understands clearly the state of the palace in 1423. The works of addition or renovation had now been proceeding, at intervals, during a space of a hundred and twenty-three years. Three generations at least had been accustomed to witness the gradual advancement of the form of the Ducal Palace into more stately symmetry, and to contrast the work of sculpture and painting with which it was decorated,—full of the life, knowledge, and hope of the fourteenth century,—with the rude Byzantine chiselling of the palace of the Doge Ziani. The magnificent fabric just completed, of which the new Council Chamber was the nucleus, was now habitually known in Venice as the "Palazzo Nuovo;" and the old Byzantine edifice, now ruinous, and more manifest in its decay by its contrast with the goodly stones of the building which had been raised at its side, was of course known as the "Palazzo Vecchio."* That fabric, however, still occupied the principal position in Venice. The new Council Chamber had been erected by the

* Baseggio (Pareri, p. 127) is called the Proto of the *New* Palace. Farther notes will be found in Appendix 1, Vol. III.

side of it towards the sea; but there was not
then the wide quay in front, the Riva de'
Schiavoni, which now renders the Sea Façade
as important as that to the Piazzetta.   There
was only a narrow walk between the pillars and
the water; and the *old* palace of Ziani still faced
the Piazzetta, and interrupted, by its decrepitude,
the magnificence of the square where the nobles
daily met.   Every increase of the beauty of the
new palace rendered the discrepancy between it
and the companion building more painful; and
then began to arise in the minds of all men a
vague idea of the necessity of destroying the old
palace, and completing the front of the Piazzetta
with the same splendour as the Sea Façade.
But no such sweeping measure of renovation
had been contemplated by the Senate when
they first formed the plan of their new Council
Chamber.   First a single additional room, then
a gateway, then a larger room; but all considered merely as necessary additions to the
palace, not as involving the entire reconstruction
of the ancient edifice.   The exhaustion of the
treasury, and the shadows upon the political
horizon, rendered it more than imprudent to
incur the vast additional expense which such a
project involved; and the Senate, fearful of itself,
and desirous to guard against the weakness of
its own enthusiasm, passed a decree, like the
effort of a man fearful of some strong temptation

to keep his thoughts averted from the point of danger. It was a decree, not merely that the old palace should not be rebuilt, but that no one should *propose* rebuilding it. The feeling of the desirableness of doing so was too strong to permit fair discussion, and the Senate knew that to bring forward such a motion was to carry it.

§ XXI. The decree, thus passed in order to guard against their own weakness, forbade any one to speak of rebuilding the old palace, under the penalty of a thousand ducats. But they had rated their own enthusiasm too low: there was a man among them whom the loss of a thousand ducats could not deter from proposing what he believed to be for the good of the state.

Some excuse was given him for bringing forward the motion by a fire which occurred in 1419, and which injured both the Church of St. Mark's, and part of the old palace fronting the Piazzetta. What followed, I shall relate in the words of Sanuto.*

§ XXII. "Therefore they set themselves with all diligence and care to repair and adorn sumptuously, first God's house; but in the Prince's house things went on more slowly, for *it did not please the Doge†* to restore it in the *form in which it was before;* and they could not

---

* Cronaca Sanudo, No. CXXV. in the Marcian Library, p. 568.

† Tomaso Mocenigo.

rebuild it altogether in a better manner, so great
was the parsimony of these old fathers; because
it was forbidden by laws, which condemned in a
penalty of a thousand ducats any one who should
propose to throw down the *old* palace, and to
rebuild it more richly and with greater expense.
But the Doge, who was magnanimous, and who
desired above all things what was honourable to
the city, had the thousand ducats carried into
the Senate Chamber, and then proposed that the
palace should be rebuilt; saying, that, ' since
the late fire had ruined in great part the Ducal
habitation (not only his own private palace, but
all the places used for public business), this
occasion was to be taken for an admonishment
sent from God, that they ought to rebuild the
palace more nobly, and in a way more befitting
the greatness to which, by God's grace, their
dominions had reached; and that his motive in
proposing this was neither ambition, nor selfish
interest: that, as for ambition, they might have
seen in the whole course of his life, through so
many years, that he had never done anything
for ambition, either in the city, or in foreign
business; but in all his actions had kept justice
first in his thoughts, and then the advantage
of the state, and the honour of the Venetian
name: and that, as far as regarded his private
interest, if it had not been for this accident
of the fire, he would never have thought of

changing anything in the palace into either a
more sumptuous or a more honourable form;
and that during the many years in which he had
lived in it, he had never endeavoured to make
any change, but had always been content with
it as his predecessors had left it; and that he
knew well that, if they took in hand to build it
as he exhorted and besought them, being now
very old, and broken down with many toils, God
would call him to another life before the walls
were raised a pace from the ground. And that
therefore they might perceive that he did not
advise them to raise this building for his own
convenience, but only for the honour of the city
and its dukedom; and that the good of it would
never be felt by him, but by his successors.'
Then he said, that 'in order, as he had always
done, to observe the laws, . . . he had brought
with him the thousand ducats which had been
appointed as the penalty for proposing such a
measure, so that he might prove openly to all
men that it was not his own advantage that he
sought, but the dignity of the state.'" There
was no one (Sanuto goes on to tell us) who
ventured, or desired, to oppose the wishes of
the Doge; and the thousand ducats were unanimously devoted to the expenses of the work.
"And they set themselves with much diligence to
the work; and the palace was begun in the form
and manner in which it is at present seen; but,

as Mocenigo had prophesied, not long after, he ended his life, and not only did not see the work brought to a close, but hardly even begun."

§ XXIII.   There are one or two expressions in the above extracts which, if they stood alone, might lead the reader to suppose that the whole palace had been thrown down and rebuilt. We must however remember, that, at this time, the new Council Chamber, which had been one hundred years in building, was actually unfinished, the Council had not yet sat in it; and it was just as likely that the Doge should then propose to destroy and rebuild it, as in this year, 1853, it is that any one should propose in our House of Commons to throw down the new Houses of Parliament, under the title of the " old palace," and rebuild *them*.

§ XXIV.   The manner in which Sanuto expresses himself will at once be seen to be perfectly natural, when it is remembered that although we now speak of the whole building as the " Ducal Palace," it consisted, in the minds of the old Venetians, of four distinct buildings. There were in it the palace, the state prisons, the senate-house, and the offices of public business; in other words, it was Buckingham Palace, the Tower of olden days, the Houses of Parliament, and Downing Street, all in one; and any of these four portions might be spoken of, without involving an allusion to any other. " Il Palazzo " was the

Ducal residence, which, with most of the public
offices, Mocenigo *did* propose to pull down and
rebuild, and which was actually pulled down
and rebuilt.   But the new Council Chamber, of
which the whole façade to the Sea consisted,
never entered into either his or Sanuto's mind
for an instant, as necessarily connected with the
Ducal residence.

I said that the new Council Chamber, at the
time when Mocenigo brought forward his measure,
had never yet been used.   It was in the year
1422 * that the decree passed to rebuild the
palace : Mocenigo died in the following year,†
and Francesco Foscari was elected in his room.
The Great Council Chamber was used for the
first time on the day when Foscari entered the
Senate as Doge,—the 3rd of April, 1423, according to the Caroldo Chronicle ; ‡ the 23rd, which
is probably correct, by anonymous MS., No. 60,
in the Correr Museum ; §—and, the following

* Vide notes in Appendix (old edition).

† On the 4th of April, 1423, according to the copy of the
Zancarol Chronicle in the Marcian Library, but previously,
according to the Caroldo Chronicle, which makes Foscari enter
the Senate as Doge on the 3rd of April.

‡ "Nella quale (the sala del Gran Consiglio) non si fece
Gran Consiglio salvo nell' anno 1423, alli 3 April, et fu il primo
giorno che il Duce Foscari venisse in Gran Consiglio dopo la
sua creatione."—Copy in Marcian Library, p. 365.

§ " E a di 23 April (1423, by the context) sequente fo fatto
Gran Conseio in la salla nuova dovi avanti non esta piu fatto
Gran Conseio si che el primo Gran Conseio dope la sua

year, on the 27th of March, the first hammer was lifted up against the old palace of Ziani.*

§ xxv. That hammer stroke was the first act of the period properly called the "Renaissance." It was the knell of the architecture of Venice,— and of Venice herself.

The central epoch of her life was past; the decay had already begun : I dated its commencement above (Ch. I. Vol. I.) from the death of Mocenigo. A year had not yet elapsed since that great Doge had been called to his account : his patriotism, always sincere, had been in this instance mistaken ; in his zeal for the honour of future Venice, he had forgotten what was due to the Venice of long ago. A thousand palaces might be built upon her burdened islands, but none of them could take the place, or recall the memory, of that which was first built upon her unfrequented shore. It fell; and, as if it had been the talisman of her fortunes, the city never flourished again.

§ xxvi. I have no intention of following out, in their intricate details, the operations which were begun under Foscari, and continued under succeeding Doges, till the palace assumed its present form, for I am not in this work concerned, except by occasional reference, with the

(Foscari's creation) fo fatto in la salla nuova, nel qual conseie fu el Marchese di Mantoa," etc., p. 426.

* Compare Appendix 1, Vol. III. (old edition).

architecture of the fifteenth century: but the main facts are the following. The Palace of Ziani was destroyed; the existing façade to the Piazzetta built, so as both to continue and to resemble, in most particulars, the work of the Great Council Chamber. It was carried back from the Sea as far as the Judgment angle; beyond which is the Porta della Carta, begun in 1439, and finished in two years, under the Doge Foscari; * the interior buildings connected with it were added by the Doge Christopher Moro (the Othello of Shakespeare)† in 1462.

§ XXVII. By reference to the figure the reader will see that we have now gone the round of the palace, and that the new work of 1462 was close upon the first piece of the Gothic Palace, the *new* Council Chamber of 1301. Some remnants of the Ziani Palace were perhaps still left between the two extremities of the Gothic Palace; or, as is more probable, the last stones of it may have been swept away after the fire of

---

* "Tutte queste fatture si compirono sotto il dogado de Foscari, nel 1441."—*Pareri*, p. 131.

† This identification has been accomplished, and I think conclusively, by my friend Mr. Rawdon Brown, who has devoted all the leisure which, during the last twenty years, his manifold offices of kindness to almost every English visitant of Venice have left him, in discovering and translating the passages of the Venetian records which bear upon English history and literature. I shall have occasion to take advantage hereafter of a portion of his labours, which I trust will shortly be made public.

1419, and replaced by new apartments for the
Doge. But whatever buildings, old or new,
stood on this spot at the time of the completion of the Porta della Carta were destroyed
by another great fire in 1479, together with so
much of the palace on the Rio that, though the
saloon of Gradenigo, then known as the Sala de'
Pregadi, was not destroyed, it became necessary
to reconstruct the entire façades of the portion
of the palace behind the Bridge of Sighs, both
towards the court and canal. This work was
entrusted to the best Renaissance architects of
the close of the fifteenth and opening of the
sixteenth centuries; Antonio Ricci executing the
Giant's staircase, and, on his absconding with a
large sum of the public money, Pietro Lombardo
taking his place. The whole work must have
been completed towards the middle of the sixteenth century. The architects of the palace
advancing round the square and led by fire,
had more than reached the point from which
they had set out; and the work of 1560 was
joined to the work of 1301—1340, at the
point marked by the letter A, Fig. II., on the
Rio Façade.

§ XXVIII. But the palace was not long permitted to remain in this finished form. Another
terrific fire, commonly called the great fire, burst
out in 1574, and destroyed the inner fittings and
all the precious pictures of the Great Council

Chamber, and of all the upper rooms on the Sea
Façade, and most of those on the Rio Façade,
leaving the building a mere shell, shaken and
blasted by the flames. It was debated in the
Great Council whether the ruin should not be
thrown down and an entirely new palace built
in its stead. The opinions of all the leading architects of Venice were taken respecting the safety
of the walls, or the possibility of repairing them
as they stood. These opinions, given in writing,
have been preserved, and published by the Abbé
Cadorin, in the work already so often referred to ;
and they form one of the most important series
of documents connected with the Ducal Palace.

I cannot help feeling some childish pleasure in
the accidental resemblance to my own name in
that of the architect whose opinion was first
given in favour of the ancient fabric, Giovanni
Rusconi. Others, especially Palladio, wanted to
pull down the old palace and execute designs of
their own ; but the best architects in Venice,
and, to his immortal honour, chiefly Francesco
Sansovino, energetically pleaded for the Gothic
pile, and prevailed. It was successfully repaired, and Tintoret painted his noblest picture
on the wall from which the " Paradise " of
Guariento had withered before the flames.

§ XXIX. The repairs necessarily undertaken at
this time were however extensive, and interfere
in many directions with the earlier work of the

palace: still the only serious alteration in its
form was the transposition of the prisons, formerly at the top of the palace, to the other side
of the Rio del Palazzo; and the building of the
Bridge of Sighs, to connect them with the palace,
by Antonio da Ponte. The completion of this
work brought the whole edifice into its present
form; with the exception of alterations in doors,
partitions, and staircases among the inner apartments not worth noticing, and such barbarisms
and defacements as have been suffered within
the last fifty years, by, I suppose, nearly every
building of importance in Italy.

§ xxx. Now, therefore, we are at liberty to
examine some of the details of the Ducal Palace,
without any doubt about their dates. I shall
not, however, give any elaborate illustrations of
them here, because I could not do them justice
on the scale of the page of this volume, or by
means of line engraving. I believe a new era
is opening to us in the art of illustration,* and
that I shall be able to give permanent photographs of the details of the Ducal Palace at
a price which will enable every person who is
interested in the subject to possess them; so
that the cost and labour of multiplying illustrations here would be altogether wasted. I
shall therefore direct the reader's attention only

* See in the old edition the last chapter of the third volume.

to such points of interest as can be explained in the text.

§ XXXI. First, then, looking back to Fig. I., the reader will observe that, as the building was very nearly square on the ground plan, a peculiar prominence and importance were given to its angles, which rendered it necessary that they should be enriched and softened by sculpture. I do not suppose that the fitness of this arrangement will be questioned; but if the reader will take the pains to glance over any series of engravings of church towers or other four-square buildings in which great refinement of form has been attained, he will at once observe how their effect depends on some modification of the sharpness of the angle, either by groups of buttresses, or by turrets and niches rich in sculpture. It is to be noted also that this principle of breaking the angle is peculiarly Gothic, arising partly out of the necessity of strengthening the flanks of enormous buildings, where composed of imperfect materials, by buttresses or pinnacles; partly out of the conditions of Gothic warfare, which generally required a tower at the angle; partly out of the natural dislike of the meagreness of effect in buildings which admitted large surfaces of wall, if the angle were entirely unrelieved. The Ducal Palace, in its acknowledgment of this principle, makes a more definite concession to the Gothic spirit than any of the previous

architecture of Venice. No angle, up to the
time of its erection, had been otherwise decorated
than by a narrow fluted pilaster of red marble,
and the sculpture was reserved always, as in Greek
and Roman work, for the plane surfaces of the
building, with, as far as I recollect, two excep-
tions only, both in St. Mark's; namely, the bold
and grotesque gargoyle on its north-west angle,
and the angles which project from the four inner
angles under the main cupola; both of these
arrangements being plainly made under Lombardic influence. And if any other instances
occur, which I may have at present forgotten,
I am very sure the Northern influence will
always be distinctly traceable in them.

§ XXXII. The Ducal Palace, however, accepts
the principle in its completeness, and throws the
main decoration upon its angles. The central
window, which looks rich and important in the
woodcut, was entirely restored in the Renaissance
time, as we have seen, under the Doge Steno;
so that we have no traces of its early treatment,
and the principal interest of the older palace is
concentrated in the angle sculpture, which is
arranged in the following manner. The pillars
of the two bearing arcades are much enlarged in
thickness at the angles, and their capitals increased in depth, breadth, and fulness of subject;
above each capital, on the angle of the wall, a
sculptural subject is introduced, consisting, in

the great lower arcade, of two or more figures of the size of life; in the upper arcade, of a single angel holding a scroll; above these angels rise the twisted pillars with their crowning niches; thus forming an unbroken line of decoration from the ground to the top of the angle.

§ XXXIII. It was before noticed that one of the corners of the palace joins the irregular outer buildings connected with St. Mark's, and is not generally seen. There remain, therefore, to be decorated, only the three angles, above distinguished as the Vine angle, the Fig-tree angle, and the Judgment angle; and at these we have, according to the arrangement just explained,—

First, Three great bearing capitals (lower arcade).

Secondly, Three figure subjects of sculpture above them (lower arcade).

Thirdly, Three smaller bearing capitals (upper arcade).

Fourthly, Three angels above them (upper arcade).

Fifthly, Three spiral shafts with niches.

§ XXXIV. I shall describe the bearing capitals hereafter, in their order, with the others of the arcade; for the first point to which the reader's attention ought to be directed is the choice of subject in the great figure sculptures above

them. These, observe, are the very corner-
stones of the edifice, and in them we may
expect to find the most important evidences of
the feeling, as well as of the skill, of the
builder. If he has anything to say to us of
the purpose with which he built the palace, it
is sure to be said here; if there was any lesson
which he wished principally to teach to those
for whom he built, here it is sure to be incul-
cated : if there was any sentiment which they
themselves desired to have expressed in the
principal edifice of their city, this is the place
in which we may be secure of finding it legibly
inscribed.

§ xxxv. Now, the first two angles, of the
Vine and Fig-tree, belong to the old, or true
Gothic, Palace; the third angle belongs to the
Renaissance imitation of it : therefore, at the
first two angles, it is the Gothic Spirit which
is going to speak to us; and, at the third, the
Renaissance spirit.

The reader remembers, I trust, that the most
characteristic sentiment of all that we traced
in the working of the Gothic heart, was the
frank confession of its own weakness; and I
must anticipate, for a moment, the results of
our inquiry in subsequent chapters, so far
as to state that the principal element in the
Renaissance spirit, is its firm confidence in its
own wisdom.

Here, then, the two spirits speak for themselves.

The first main sculpture of the Gothic Palace
is on what I have called the angle of the Fig-
tree :

Its subject is the FALL OF MAN.

The second sculpture is on the angle of the
Vine :

Its subject is the DRUNKENNESS OF NOAH.

The Renaissance sculpture is on the Judgment
angle :

Its subject is the JUDGMENT OF SOLOMON.

It is impossible to overstate, or to regard with
too much admiration, the significance of this
single fact.   It is as if the palace had been built
at various epochs, and preserved uninjured to
this day, for the sole purpose of teaching us the
difference in the temper of the two schools.

§ XXXVI. I have called the sculpture on the
Fig-tree angle the principal one ; because it is
at the central bend of the palace, where it turns
to the Piazzetta (the façade upon the Piazzetta,
being, as we saw above, the more important
one in ancient times).   The great capital, which
sustains this Fig-tree angle, is also by far more
elaborate than the head of the pilaster under
the Vine angle, marking the pre-eminence of the
former in the architect's mind.   It is impossible
to say which was first executed, but that of the
Fig-tree angle is somewhat rougher in execution,

and more stiff in the design of the figures, so
that I rather suppose it to have been the earliest
completed.

§ XXXVII. In both the subjects, of the Fall
and the Drunkenness, the tree, which forms the
chiefly decorative portion of the sculpture,—fig
in the one case, vine in the other,—was a
necessary adjunct. Its trunk, in both sculptures,
forms the true outer angle of the palace; boldly
cut separate from the stonework behind, and
branching out above the figures so as to enwrap
each side of the angle, for several feet, with its
deep foliage. Nothing can be more masterly or
superb than the sweep of this foliage on the Fig-
tree angle; the broad leaves lapping round the
budding fruit, and sheltering from sight, beneath
their shadows, birds of the most graceful form
and delicate plumage. The branches are, however, so strong, and the masses of stone hewn
into leafage so large, that, notwithstanding the
depth of the undercutting, the work remains
nearly uninjured; not so at the Vine angle,
where the natural delicacy of the vine-leaf and
tendril having tempted the sculptor to greater
effort, he has passed the proper limits of his art,
and cut the upper stems so delicately that half
of them have been broken away by the casualties
to which the situation of the sculpture necessarily
exposes it. What remains is, however, so interesting in its extreme refinement, that I have

chosen it for the subject of the first illustration*
rather than the nobler masses of the fig-tree
which ought to be rendered on a larger scale.
Although half of the beauty of the composition
is destroyed by the breaking away of its central
masses, there is still enough in the distribution of
the variously bending leaves, and in the placing
of the birds on the lighter branches, to prove to
us the power of the designer. I have already
referred to this plate as a remarkable instance of
the Gothic Naturalism; and, indeed, it is almost
impossible for the copying of nature to be carried
further than in the fibres of the marble branches,
and the careful finishing of the tendrils : note
especially the peculiar expression of the knotty
joints of the vine in the light branch which rises
highest. Yet only half the finish of the work
can be seen in the plate : for, in several cases, the
sculptor has shown the under sides of the leaves
turned boldly to the light, and has literally
carved every rib and vein upon them in relief;
not merely the main ribs which sustain the lobes
of the leaf, and actually project in nature, but
the irregular and sinuous veins which chequer the
membranous tissues between them, and which
the sculptor has represented conventionally as
relieved like the others, in order to give the vine-
leaf its peculiar tesselated effect upon the eye.

§ XXXVIII. As must always be the case in

* See note at end of this chapter.

early sculpture, the figures are much inferior to
the leafage ; yet so skilful in many respects, that
it was a long time before I could persuade myself
that they had indeed been wrought in the first
half of the fourteenth century. Fortunately,
the date is inscribed upon a monument in the
Church of San Simeon Grande, bearing a recumbent statue of the saint, of far finer workmanship, in every respect, than those figures of the
Ducal Palace, yet so like them, that I think there
can be no question that the head of Noah was
wrought by the sculptor of the palace in emulation of that of the statue of St. Simeon. In
this latter sculpture, the face is represented in
death ; the mouth partly open, the lips thin and
sharp, the teeth carefully sculptured beneath ;
the face full of quietness and majesty, though
very ghastly ; the hair and beard flowing in
luxuriant wreaths, disposed with the most
masterly freedom, yet severity, of design, far
down upon the shoulders ; the hands crossed
upon the body, carefully studied, and the veins
and sinews perfectly and easily expressed, yet
without any attempt at extreme finish or display of technical skill. This monument bears
date 1317,* and its sculptor was justly proud of
it ; thus recording his name:

* "In XRI—NOIE AMEN ANNINCARNATIONIS MCCCXVII.
INESETBR." "In the name of Christ, Amen, in the year of
the incarnation, 1317, in the month of September," etc.

"Celavit Marcus opus hoc insigne Romanis,
Laudibus non parcus est sua digna manus."

§ xxxix. The head of the Noah on the Ducal
Palace, evidently worked in emulation of this
statue, has the same profusion of flowing hair
and beard, but wrought in smaller and harder
curls; and the veins on the arms and breast are
more sharply drawn, the sculptor being evidently
more practised in keen and fine lines of vegetation than in those of the figure; so that, which
is most remarkable in a workman of this early
period, he has failed in telling his story plainly,
regret and wonder being so equally marked on
the features of all the three brothers, that it
is impossible to say which is intended for Ham.
Two of the heads of the brothers are seen in the
plate; the third figure is not with the rest of
the group, but set at a distance of about twelve
feet, on the other side of the arch which springs
from the angle capital.

§ xl. It may be observed, as a farther evidence
of the date of the group, that, in the figures of
all the three youths, the feet are protected simply
by a bandage arranged in crossed folds round
the ankle and lower part of the limb; a feature
of dress which will be found in nearly every
piece of figure sculpture in Venice, from the year
1300 to 1380, and of which the traveller may
see an example within three hundred yards of
this very group, in the bas-reliefs on the tomb of

the Doge Andrea Dandolo (in St. Mark's), who
died in 1354.

§ XLI. The figures of Adam and Eve, sculptured on each side of the Fig-tree angle, are
more stiff than those of Noah and his sons, but
are better fitted for their architectural service;
and the trunk of the tree, with the angular body
of the serpent writhed around it, is more nobly
treated as a terminal group of lines than that
of the vine.

The Renaissance sculptor of the figures of the
Judgment of Solomon has very nearly copied the
fig-tree from this angle, placing its trunk between
the executioner and the mother, who leans forward to stay his hand. But, though the whole
group is much more free in design than those of
the earlier palace, and in many ways excellent
in itself, so that it always strikes the eye of a
careless observer more than the others, it is of
immeasurably inferior spirit in the workmanship; the leaves of the tree, though far more
studiously varied in flow than those of the fig-
tree from which they are partially copied, have
none of its truth to nature; they are ill set on
the stems, bluntly defined on the edges, and their
curves are not those of growing leaves, but of
wrinkled drapery.

§ XLII. Above these three sculptures are set,
in the upper arcade, the statues of the archangels
Raphael, Michael, and Gabriel: their positions

will be understood by reference to the lowest
figure in Plate XVII., where that of Raphael
above the Vine angle is seen on the right. A
diminutive figure of Tobit follows at his feet,
and he bears in his hand a scroll with this inscription :—

EFICE Q̄
SOFRE
TUR AFA
EL REVE
RENDE
QUIETŪ

i.e., Effice (quæso ?) fretum, Raphael reverende,
quietum.* I could not decipher the inscription
on the scroll borne by the angel Michael ; † and
the figure of Gabriel, which is by much the most
beautiful feature of the Renaissance portion of
the palace, has only in its hand the Annunciation
lily.

§ XLIII. Such are the subjects of the main

---

* "Oh, venerable Raphael, make thou the gulf calm, we
beseech thee." The peculiar office of the angel Raphael is, in
general, according to tradition, the restraining the harmful
influences of evil spirits. Sir Charles Eastlake told me, that
sometimes in this office he is represented bearing the gall of
the fish caught by Tobit ; and reminded me of the peculiar
superstitions of the Venetians respecting the raising of storms
by fiends, as embodied in the well-known tale of the Fisherman
and St. Mark's ring.

† [It was, however, lately (1884) read by a correspondent,
thus :—" Ense bonos tego, malorum crimina purgo."]

sculptures decorating the angles of the palace;
notable, observe, for their simple expression of
two feelings, the consciousness of human frailty,
and the dependence upon Divine guidance and
protection; this being, of course, the general
purpose of the introduction of the figures of the
angels; and, I imagine, intended to be more
particularly conveyed by the manner in which
the small figure of Tobit follows the steps of
Raphael just touching the hem of his garment.
We have next to examine the course of divinity
and of natural history embodied by the old
sculptor in the great series of capitals which
support the lower arcade of the palace; and
which, being at a height of little more than eight
feet above the eye, might be read, like the pages
of a book, by those (the noblest men in Venice)
who habitually walked beneath the shadow of this
great arcade at the time of their first meeting
each other for morning converse.

§ LXV.[a] It has already been mentioned (Chap.
I. § XLVI.) that there are, in all, thirty-six great
pillars supporting the lower story; and that these
are to be counted from right to left, because then
the more ancient of them come first: and that,
thus arranged, the first, which is not a shaft, but
a pilaster, will be the support of the Vine angle;
the eighteenth will be the great shaft of the

---

[a] [Paragraphs XLIV.—LXIV. of this chapter in the old
edition are here omitted.]

Fig-tree angle ; and the thirty-sixth, that of the Judgment angle.

All their capitals, except that of the first, are octagonal, and are decorated by sixteen leaves, differently enriched in every capital, but arranged in the same way; eight of them rising to the angles, and there forming volutes; the eight others set between them, on the sides, rising half-way up the bell of the capital; there nodding forward, and showing above them, rising out of their luxuriance, the groups or single figures which we have to examine.* In some instances, the intermediate or lower leaves are reduced to eight sprays of foliage; and the capital is left dependent for its effect on the bold position of the figures. In referring to the figures on the octagonal capitals I shall call the outer side, fronting either the Sea or the Piazzetta, the first side ; and so count round from left to right; the fourth side being thus, of course, the innermost. As, however, the first five arches were walled up after the great fire, only three sides of their capitals are left visible, which we may describe as the front and the eastern and western sides of each.

---

* I have given one of these capitals carefully already in my folio work, and hope to give most of the others in due time. It was of no use to draw them here, as the scale would have been too small to allow me to show the expression of the figures.

§ LXVI. FIRST CAPITAL : *i.e.*, of the pilaster at the Vine angle.

In front, towards the Sea. A child holding a bird before him, with its wings expanded, covering his breast.

On its eastern side. Children's heads among leaves.

On its western side. A child carrying in one hand a comb; in the other a pair of scissors.

It appears curious, that this, the principal pilaster of the façade, should have been decorated only by these graceful grotesques, for I can hardly suppose them anything more. There may be meaning in them, but I will not venture to conjecture any, except the very plain and practical meaning conveyed by the last figure to all Venetian children, which it would be well if they would act upon. For the rest, I have seen the comb introduced in grotesque work as early as the thirteenth century, but generally for the purpose of ridiculing too great care in dressing the hair, which assuredly is not its purpose here. The children's heads are very sweet and full of life, but the eyes sharp and small.

§ LXVII. SECOND CAPITAL. Only three sides of the original work are left unburied by the mass of added wall. Each side has a bird, one web-footed, with a fish; one clawed, with a serpent, which opens its jaws, and darts its tongue at the bird's breast; the third pluming itself, with a feather between the mandibles of its bill. It is by far the most beautiful of the three capitals decorated with birds.

THIRD CAPITAL. Also has three sides only left. They have three heads, large and very ill cut; one female, and crowned.

FOURTH CAPITAL. Has three children. The eastern one is defaced: the one in front holds a small bird, whose plumage is beautifully indicated, in its right hand; and with its left holds up half a walnut, showing the nut inside: the third holds a fresh fig, cut through, showing the seeds.

The hair of all the three children is differently worked; the first has luxuriant flowing hair, and a double chin: the second, light flowing hair falling in pointed locks on the forehead; the third, crisp curling hair, deep cut with drill holes.

This capital has been copied on the Renaissance side of the palace, only with such changes in the ideal of the children as the workman thought expedient and natural. It is highly interesting to compare the child of the fourteenth with the child of the fifteenth century. The early heads are full of youthful life, playful, humane, affectionate, beaming with sensation and vivacity, but with much manliness and

firmness also, not a little cunning, and some
cruelty perhaps, beneath all; the features small
and hard, and the eyes keen. There is the
making of rough and great men in them. But
the children of the fifteenth century are dull
smooth-faced dunces, without a single meaning
line in the fatness of their stolid cheeks; and,
although, in the vulgar sense, as handsome as
the other children are ugly, capable of becoming
nothing but perfumed coxcombs.

FIFTH CAPITAL. Still three sides only left,
bearing three half-length statues of kings; this
is the first capital which bears any inscription.
In front, a king with a sword in his right hand
points to a handkerchief embroidered and
fringed, with a head on it, carved on the cavetto
of the abacus. His name is written above,
"TITUS VESPASIAN IMPERATOR" (contracted

I𝚿AT).

On eastern side, "TRAJANUS IMPERATOR."
Crowned, a sword in right hand, and sceptre in left.

On western, "(OCT) AVIANUS AUGUSTUS
IMPERATOR." The "OCT" is broken away. He
bears a globe in his right hand, with "MUNDUS
PACIS" upon it; a sceptre in his left, which I
think has terminated in a human figure. He
has a flowing beard, and a singularly high
crown; the face is much injured, but has once
been very noble in expression.

SIXTH CAPITAL. Has large male and female heads, very coarsely cut, hard, and bad.

§ LXVIII. SEVENTH CAPITAL. This is the first of the series which is complete; the first open arch of the lower arcade being between it and the sixth. It begins the representation of the Virtues.

First side. Largitas, or Liberality: always distinguished from the higher Charity. A male figure, with his lap full of money, which he pours out of his hand. The coins are plain, circular, and smooth; there is no attempt to mark device upon them. The inscription above is, "LARGITAS ME ONORAT."

In the copy of this design on the twenty-fifth capital, instead of showering out the gold from his open hand, the figure holds it in a plate or salver, introduced for the sake of disguising the direct imitation. The changes thus made in the Renaissance pillars are always injuries.

This virtue is the proper opponent of Avarice; though it does not occur in the systems of Orcagna or Giotto, being included in Charity. It was a leading virtue with Aristotle and the other ancients.

§ LXIX. *Second side.* Constancy; not very characteristic. An armed man with a sword in his hand, inscribed, "CONSTANTIA SUM, NIL TIMENS."

This virtue is one of the forms of fortitude,

and Giotto therefore sets as the vice opponent to Fortitude, "Inconstantia," represented as a woman in loose drapery, falling from a rolling globe. The vision seen in the interpreter's house in the 'Pilgrim's Progress,' of the man with a very bold countenance, who says to him who has the writer's ink-horn by his side, "Set down my name," is the best personification of the Venetian "Constantia" of which I am aware in literature. It would be well for us all to consider whether we have yet given the order to the man with the ink-horn, "Set down my name."

§ LXX. *Third side.* Discord; holding up her finger, but needing the inscription above to assure us of her meaning, "DISCORDIA SUM, DISCORDANS." In the Renaissance copy she is a meek and nun-like person with a veil.

She is the Atë of Spenser: "mother of debate," thus inscribed in the fourth book :—

> "Her face most fowle and filthy was to see,
>   With squinted eyes contrarie wayes intended ;
>   And loathly mouth, unmeete a mouth to bee,
>   That nought but gall and venim comprehended,
>   And wicked words that God and man offended :
>   Her lying tongue was in two parts divided,
>   And both the parts did speake, and both contended ;
>   And as her tongue, so was her hart discided,
>   That never thoght one thing, but doubly stil was guided."

Note the fine old meaning of "discided," cut in two; it is a great pity we have lost this powerful expression. We might keep "determined" for the other sense of the word.

§ LXXI. *Fourth side.* Patience. A female figure, very expressive and lovely, in a hood, with her right hand on her breast, the left extended, inscribed "PATIENTIA MANET MECUM."

She is one of the principal virtues in all the Christian systems, a masculine virtue in Spenser, and beautifully placed as the *Physician* in the House of Holinesse. The opponent vice, Impatience, is one of the hags who attend the Captain of the lusts of the Flesh; the other being Impotence. In like manner, in the 'Pilgrim's Progress,' the opposite of Patience is Passion; but Spenser's thought is farther carried. His two hags, Impatience and Impotence, as attendant upon the evil spirit of Passion, embrace all the phenomena of human conduct, down even to the smallest matters, according to the adage, "More haste, worse speed."

§ LXXII. *Fifth side.* Despair. A female figure thrusting a dagger into her throat, and tearing her long hair, which flows down among the leaves of the capital below her knees. One of the finest figures of the series; inscribed "DESPERACIO MÓꙗ (motis?) CRUDELIS." In the Renaissance copy she is totally devoid of expression, and appears, instead of tearing her hair, to be dividing it into long curls on each side.

This vice is the proper opposite of Hope. By
Giotto she is represented as a woman hanging
herself, a fiend coming for her soul. Spenser's
vision of Despair is well known, it being indeed
currently reported that this part of the 'Faerie
Queen' was the first which drew to it the attention of Sir Philip Sidney.

§ LXXIII. *Sixth side.* Obedience; with her
arms folded; meek, but rude and commonplace,
looking at a little dog standing on its hind legs
and begging, with a collar round its neck. Inscribed " OBEDIENTI * * ;" the rest of the sentence
is much defaced, but looks like ΛΌῆΟᗺΧΙℬᗺΟ.
I suppose the note of contraction above the
final A has disappeared, and that the inscription
was "Obedientium domino exhibeo."

This virtue is, of course, a principal one in
the monkish systems; represented by Giotto
at Assisi as " an angel robed in black, placing
the finger of his left hand on his mouth, and
passing the yoke over the head of a Franciscan
monk kneeling at his feet." *

Obedience holds a less principal place in
Spenser. We have seen her above associated
with the other peculiar virtues of womanhood.

§ LXXIV. *Seventh side.* Infidelity. A man in
a turban, with a small image in his hand, or the
image of a child. Of the inscription nothing

---

* Lord Lindsay, vol. ii. p. 226.

but "INFIDELITATE * * *" and some fragmentary letters, "ILI, CERO," remain.

By Giotto Infidelity is most nobly symbolised as a woman helmeted, the helmet having a broad rim which keeps the light from her eyes. She is covered with a heavy drapery, stands infirmly as if about to fall, is *bound by a cord round her neck to an image* which she carries in her hand, and has flames bursting forth at her feet.

In Spenser, Infidelity is the Saracen knight Sans Foy,—

> " Full large of limbe and every joint
> He was, and cared not for God or man a point."

For the part which he sustains in the contest with Godly Fear, or the Red-cross Knight, see Appendix II., Vol. III.

§ LXXV. *Eighth side.* Modesty ; bearing a pitcher. (In the Renaissance copy, a vase like a coffee-pot.) Inscribed "MODESTIA ꝶOBUOBTIꝺꝺo."

I do not find this virtue in any of the Italian series, except that of Venice. In Spenser she is of course one of those attendant on Womanhood, but occurs as one of the tenants of the heart of Man, thus portrayed in the second book :

> " Straunge was her tyre, and all her garments blew,
> Close rownd about her tuckt with many a plight ;
> Upon her fist the bird which shonneth vew.

*   *   *   *   *   *

And ever and anone with rosy red
The bashfull blood her snowy cheekes did dye,
That her became, as polisht yvory
Which cunning craftesman hand hath overlayd
With fayre vermilion or pure castory."

§ LXXVI. EIGHTH CAPITAL. It has no inscriptions, and its subjects are not, by themselves, intelligible : but they appear to be typical of the degradation of human instincts.

First side. A caricature of Arion on his dolphin; he wears a cap ending in a long proboscis-like horn, and plays a violin with a curious twitch of the bow and wag of the head, very graphically expressed, but still without anything approaching to the power of Northern grotesque. His dolphin has a goodly row of teeth, and the waves beat over its back.

Second side. A human figure, with curly hair and the legs of a bear ; the paws laid, with great sculptural skill, upon the foliage. It plays a violin, shaped like a guitar, with a bent double-stringed bow.

Third side. A figure with a serpent's tail and a monstrous head, founded on a Negro type, hollow-cheeked, large-lipped, and wearing a cap made of a serpent's skin, holding a fir-cone in its hand.

Fourth side. A monstrous figure, terminating below in a tortoise. It is devouring a gourd, which it grasps greedily with both hands ; it wears a cap ending in a hoofed leg.

Fifth side. A centaur wearing a crested helmet, and holding a curved sword.

Sixth side. A knight, riding a headless horse, and wearing chain armour, with a triangular shield flung behind his back, and a two-edged sword.

Seventh side. A figure like that on the fifth, wearing a round helmet, and with the legs and tail of a horse. He bears a long mace with a top like a fir-cone.

Eighth side. A figure with curly hair, and an acorn in its hand, ending below in a fish.

§ LXXVII. NINTH CAPITAL. *First side.* Faith. She has her left hand on her breast, and the cross in her right. Inscribed " FIDES OPTIMA IN DEO." The Faith of Giotto holds the cross in her right hand; in her left, a scroll with the Apostles' Creed. She treads upon cabalistic books, and has a key suspended to her waist. Spenser's Faith (Fidelia) is still more spiritual and noble :

" She was araied all in lily white,
　And in her right hand bore a cup of gold,
　With wine and water fild up to the hight,
　In which a serpent did himselfe enfold,
　That horrour made to all that did behold ;
　But she no whitt did chaunge her constant mood :
　And in her other hand she fast did hold
　A booke, that was both signd and seald with blood ;
　Wherein darke things were writt, hard to be understood."

§ LXXVIII. *Second side.* Fortitude. A long-

bearded man [Samson?] tearing open a lion's
jaw. The inscription is illegible, and the somewhat vulgar personification appears to belong
rather to Courage than Fortitude. On the
Renaissance copy it is inscribed "FORTITUDO
SUM VIRILIS." The Latin word has, perhaps,
been received by the sculptor as merely signi-
fying "Strength," the rest of the perfect idea of
this virtue having been given in "Constantia"
previously. But both these Venetian symbols
together do not at all approach the idea of
Fortitude as given generally by Giotto and the
Pisan sculptors; clothed with a lion's skin,
knotted about her neck, and falling to her feet
in deep folds; drawing back her right hand,
with the sword pointed towards her enemy; and
slightly retired behind her immovable shield,
which with Giotto is square, and rested on the
ground like a tower, covering her up to above
the shoulders; bearing on it a lion, and with
broken heads of javelins deeply infixed.

Among the Greeks, this is, of course, one of
the principal virtues; apt, however, in their
ordinary conception of it, to degenerate into
mere manliness or courage.

§ LXXIX. *Third side.* Temperance; bearing a
pitcher of water and a cup. Inscription, illegible here, and on the Renaissance copy nearly
so, "TEMPERANTIA SUM" (INÒM' L^s)? only left.
In this somewhat vulgar and most frequent

conception of this virtue (afterwards continually repeated, as by Sir Joshua in his window at New College), temperance is confused with mere abstinence, the opposite of Gula, or Gluttony; whereas the Greek temperance, a truly cardinal virtue, is the moderator of *all* the passions, and so represented by Giotto, who has placed a bridle upon her lips, and a sword in her hand, the hilt of which she is binding to the scabbard. In his system, she is opposed among the vices, not by Gula, or Gluttony, but by Ira, Anger. So also the Temperance of Spenser, or Sir Guyon, but with mingling of much sternness:—

> "A goodly knight, all armd in harnesse meete,
> That from his head no place appeared to his feete.
> His carriage was full comely and upright;
> His countenance demure and temperate;
> But yett so sterne and terrible in sight,
> That cheard his friendes, and did his foes amate."

The Temperance of the Greeks, σωφροσύνη, involves the idea of Prudence, and is a most noble virtue, yet properly marked by Plato as inferior to sacred enthusiasm, though necessary for its government. He opposes it, under the name "Mortal Temperance" or "the Temperance which is of men," to divine madness, μανία, or inspiration; but he most justly and nobly expresses the general idea of it under the term ὕβρις, which, in the "Phædrus," is divided into various intemperances with respect to various objects, and set forth under the image of a black, vicious, diseased, and furious horse, yoked by the side of Prudence or Wisdom (set forth under the figure of a white horse with a crested and noble head, like that which we have among the Elgin Marbles) to the chariot of the soul. The system of Aristotle, as above stated, is throughout a mere complicated blunder, supported by sophistry, the laboriously developed mistake of temperance for the essence of the virtues which it guides. Temperance in the mediæval systems is generally opposed by Anger, or by Folly, or Gluttony : but her proper opposite is Spenser's Acrasia, the principal enemy of Sir Guyon, at whose gates we find the subordinate vice "Excesse," as the introduction to Intemperance ; a graceful and feminine image, necessary to illustrate the more dangerous forms of subtle intemperance, as opposed to the brutal "Gluttony" in the first book. She presses grapes into a cup, because of the words of St. Paul, "Be not drunk with wine, wherein is excess;" but always delicately :

> " Into her cup she scruzd with daintie breach
> Of her fine fingers, without fowle empeach,
> That so faire winepresse made the wine more sweet."

The reader will, I trust, pardon these frequent extracts from Spenser, for it is nearly as necessary to point out the profound divinity and philosophy of our great English poet, as the beauty of the Ducal Palace.

§ LXXX. *Fourth side.* Humility; with a veil upon her head, carrying a lamb in her lap. Inscribed in the copy, "HUMILITAS HABITAT IN ME."

This virtue is of course a peculiarly Christian one, hardly recognized in the Pagan systems, though carefully impressed upon the Greeks in early life in a manner which at this day it would be well if we were to imitate, and, together with an almost feminine modesty, giving an exquisite grace to the conduct and bearing of the well-educated Greek youth. It is, of course, one of the leading virtues in all the monkish systems, but I have not any notes of the manner of its representation.

§ LXXXI. *Fifth side.* Charity. A woman with her lap full of loaves (?), giving one to a child, who stretches his arm out for it across a broad gap in the leafage of the capital.

Again very far inferior to the Giottesque rendering of this virtue. In the Arena Chapel she is distinguished from all the other virtues by having a circular glory round her head, and a cross of fire; she is crowned with flowers, presents with her right hand a vase of corn and fruit, and with her left receives treasure from Christ, who appears above her, to provide her with the means of continual offices of beneficence, while she tramples under foot the treasures of the earth.

The peculiar beauty of most of the Italian conceptions of Charity is in the subjection of mere munificence to the glowing of her love, always represented by flames; here in the form of a cross, round her head; in Orcagna's shrine at Florence, issuing from a censer in her hand; and, with Dante, inflaming her whole form, so that, in a furnace of clear fire, she could not have been discerned.

Spenser represents her as a mother surrounded by happy children, an idea afterwards grievously hackneyed and vulgarised by English painters and sculptors.

§ LXXXII. *Sixth side.* Justice. Crowned, and with sword. Inscribed in the copy " REX SUM JUSTICIE."

This idea was afterwards much amplified and adorned in the only good capital of the Renaissance series, under the Judgment angle. Giotto has also given his whole strength to the painting of this virtue, representing her as enthroned under a noble Gothic canopy, holding scales, not by the beam, but one in each hand; a beautiful idea, showing that the equality of the scales of Justice is not owing to natural laws, but to her own immediate weighing the opposed causes in her own hands. In one scale is an executioner beheading a criminal; in the other an angel crowning a man, who seems (in Selvatico's plate) to have been working at a desk or table.

Beneath her feet is a small predella, representing various persons riding securely in the woods, and others dancing to the sound of music.

Spenser's Justice, Sir Artegall, is the hero of an entire book, and the betrothed knight of Britomart, or Chastity.

§ LXXXIII. *Seventh side.* Prudence. A man with a book and a pair of compasses, wearing the noble cap, hanging down towards the shoulder, and bound in a fillet round the brow, which occurs so frequently during the fourteenth century in Italy in the portraits of men occupied in any civil capacity.

This virtue is, as we have seen, conceived under very different degrees of dignity, from mere worldly prudence up to heavenly wisdom, being opposed sometimes by Stultitia, sometimes by Ignorantia. I do not find, in any of the representations of her, that her truly distinctive character, namely *forethought,* is enough insisted upon : Giotto expresses her vigilance and just measurement or estimate of all things by painting her as Janus-headed, and gazing into a convex mirror with compasses in her right hand : the convex mirror showing her power of looking at many things in small compass. But forethought or anticipation, by which, independently of greater or less natural capacities,

one man becomes more *prudent* than another,
is never enough considered or symbolised.

The idea of this virtue oscillates, in the Greek
systems, between Temperance and Heavenly
Wisdom.

§ LXXXIV. *Eighth side.* Hope. A figure full of
devotional expression, holding up its hands as in
prayer, and looking to a hand which is extended
towards it out of sunbeams. In the Renaissance
copy this hand does not appear.

Of all the virtues, this is the most distinctively
Christian (it could not, of course, enter definitely
into any Pagan scheme); and above all others,
it seems to me the *testing* virtue,—that by the
possession of which we may most certainly
determine whether we are Christians or not;
for many men have charity, that is to say,
general kindness of heart, or even a kind of
faith, who have not any habitual *hope* of, or
longing for, heaven. The hope of Giotto is
represented as winged, rising in the air, while
an angel holds a crown before her. I do not
know if Spenser was the first to introduce our
marine Virtue leaning on an anchor, a symbol
as inaccurate as it is vulgar: for, in the first
place, anchors are not for men, but for ships;
and, in the second, anchorage is the characteristic,
not of Hope, but of Faith. Faith is dependent,
but Hope is aspirant. Spenser, however, introduces Hope twice,—the first time as the Virtue

with the anchor ; but afterwards fallacious Hope, far more beautifully, in the Masque of Cupid :—

> "She always smyled, and in her hand did hold
> An holy-water-sprinckle, dippt in deowe."

§ LXXXV. TENTH CAPITAL. *First side.* Luxury (the opposite of Chastity, as above explained). A woman with a jewelled chain across her forehead, smiling as she looks into a mirror, exposing her breast by drawing down her dress with one hand. Inscribed "LUXURIA SUM IMENSA."

These subordinate forms of vice are not met with so frequently in art as those of the opposite virtues, but in Spenser we find them all. His Luxury rides upon a goat :—

> "In a greene gowne he clothèd was full faire,
> Which underneath did hide filthinesse,
> And in his hand a burning hart he bare."

But, in fact, the proper and comprehensive expression of this vice is the Cupid of the ancients ; and there is not any minor circumstance more indicative of the *intense* difference between the mediæval and the Renaissance spirit, than the mode in which this god is represented.

I have above said, that all great European art is rooted in the thirteenth century ; and it seems to me that there is a kind of

central year about which we may consider the
energy of the middle ages to be gathered; a
kind of focus of time, which, by what is to my
mind a most touching and impressive Divine
appointment, has been marked for us by the
greatest writer of the middle-ages, in the first
words he utters; namely, the year 1300, the
" mezzo del cammin " of the life of Dante. Now,
therefore, to Giotto, the contemporary of Dante,
and who drew Dante's still existing portrait in
this very year, 1300, we may always look for
the central mediæval idea in any subject: and
observe how he represents Cupid; as one of
three, a terrible trinity, his companions being
Satan and Death; and he himself " a lean
scarecrow, with bow, quiver, and fillet, and
feet ending in claws,"* thrust down into Hell
by Penance, from the presence of Purity and
Fortitude. Spenser, who has been so often
noticed as furnishing the exactly intermediate
type of conception between the mediæval and
the Renaissance, indeed represents Cupid under
the ancient form of a beautiful winged god, and
riding on a lion, but still no plaything of the
Graces, but full of terror :—

" With that the darts which his right hand did straine
Full dreadfully he shooke, that all did quake,
And clapt on hye his colourd wingës twaine,
That all his many it afraide did make."

* Lord Lindsay, vol. ii. Letter iv.

His *many*, that is to say, his company; and observe what a company it is. Before him go Fancy, Desire, Doubt, Danger, Fear, Fallacious Hope, Dissemblance, Suspicion, Grief, Fury, Displeasure, Despite, and Cruelty. After him, Reproach, Repentance, Shame,

> " Unquiet Care, and fond Unthriftyhead,
>   Lewd Losse of Time, and Sorrow seeming dead,
>   Inconstant Chaunge, and false Disloyalty,
>   Consuming Riotise, and guilty Dread
>   Of heavenly vengeance ; faint infirmity,
>   Vile Poverty, and lastly Death with Infamy."

Compare these two pictures of Cupid with the Love-god of the Renaissance, as he is represented to this day, confused with angels, in every faded form of ornament and allegory, in our furniture, our literature, and our minds.

§ LXXXVI. *Second side.* Gluttony. A woman in a turban, with a jewelled cap in her right hand. In her left, the clawed limb of a bird, which she is gnawing. Inscribed " GULA SINE ORDINE SUM."

Spenser's Gluttony is more than usually fine :

> "His belly was upblowne with luxury,
>   And eke with fatnesse swollen were his eyne,
>   And like a crane his necke was long and fyne,
>   Wherewith he swallowed up excessive feast,
>   For want whereof poor people oft did pyne."

He rides upon a swine, and is clad in vine-leaves, with a garland of ivy. Compare the account of Excesse, above, as opposed to Temperance.

§ LXXXVII. *Third side.* Pride. A knight, with a heavy and stupid face, holding a sword with three edges; his armour covered with ornaments in the form of roses, and with two ears attached to his helmet. The inscription undecipherable, all but "SUPERBIA."

Spenser has analyzed this vice with great care. He first represents it as the Pride of Life; that is to say, the pride which runs in a deep undercurrent through all the thoughts and acts of men. As such, it is a feminine vice, directly opposed to Holiness, and mistress of a castle called the House of Pryde, and her chariot is driven by Satan, with a team of beasts, ridden by the mortal sins. In the throne chamber of her palace she is thus described:—

> " So proud she shynèd in her princely state,
> Looking to Heaven, for Earth she did disdayne;
> And sitting high, for lowly she did hate:
> Lo, underneath her scornefull feete was layne
> A dreadful dragon with an hideous trayne;
> And in her hand she held a mirrhour bright,
> Wherein her face she often vewed fayne."

The giant Orgoglio is a baser species of pride, born of the Earth and Eolus; that is to say, of sensual and vain conceits. His foster-father and the keeper of his castle is Ignorance. (Book I. Canto VIII.)

Finally, Disdain is introduced, in other places, as the form of pride which vents itself in insult to others.

§ LXXXVIII. *Fourth side.* Anger. A woman tearing her dress open at her breast. Inscription here undecipherable; but in the Renaissance copy it is " IRA CRUDELIS EST IN ME."

Giotto represents this vice under the same symbol; but it is the weakest of all the figures in the Arena Chapel. The "Wrath" of Spenser rides upon a lion, brandishing a firebrand, his garments stained with blood. Rage, or Furor, occurs subordinately in other places. It appears to me very strange that neither Giotto nor Spenser should have given any representation of the *restrained* Anger, which is infinitely the most terrible; both of them make him violent.

§ LXXXIX. *Fifth side.* Avarice. An old woman with a veil over her forehead, and a bag of money in each hand. A figure very marvellous for power of expression. The throat is all made up of sinews with skinny channels deep between them, strained as by anxiety, and wasted by famine; the features hunger-bitten, the eyes hollow, the look glaring and intense, yet without the slightest caricature. Inscribed in the Renaissance copy, " AVARITIA IMPLETOR."

Spenser's Avarice (the vice) is much feebler than this; but the God Mammon and his kingdom have been described by him with his usual

power.   Note the position of the house of
Richesse :

> "Betwixt them both was but a little stride,
>   That did the House of Richesse from Hell-mouth divide."

It is curious that most moralists confuse
avarice with covetousness, although they are
vices totally different in their operation on the
human heart and on the frame of society. The
love of money, the sin of Judas and Ananias, is
indeed the root of all evil in the hardening of
the heart ; but, " covetousness, which is idolatry,"
the sin of Ahab, that is, the inordinate desire of
some seen or recognised good,—thus destroying
peace of mind,—is probably productive of much
more misery in heart, and error in conduct, than
avarice itself, only covetousness is not so inconsistent with Christianity : for covetousness may
partly proceed from vividness of the affections
and hopes, as in David, and be consistent with
much charity ; not so avarice.

§ xc. *Sixth side.*   Idleness.   Accidia.   A
figure much broken away, having had its arms
round two branches of trees.

I do not know why Idleness should be represented as among trees, unless, in the Italy of the
fourteenth century, forest country was considered
as desert, and therefore the domain of Idleness.
Spenser fastens this vice especially upon the
clergy :

> "Upon a slouthful asse he chose to ryde,
> Arayd in habit blacke, and amis thin,
> Like to an holy monck, the service to begin,
> And in his hand his portesse still he bare,
> That much was worne, but therein little redd."

And he properly makes him the leader of the train of the vices :

> "May seem the wayne was very evil ledd,
> When such an one had guiding of the way."

Observe that subtle touch of truth in the "wearing" of the portesse, indicating the abuse of books by idle readers, so thoroughly characteristic of unwilling studentship from the schoolboy upwards.

§ XCI. *Seventh side.* Vanity. She is smiling complacently as she looks into a mirror in her lap. Her robe is embroidered with roses, and roses for her crown. Undecipherable.

There is some confusion in the expression of the vice, between pride in the personal appearance and lightness of purpose. The word Vanitas generally, I think, bears, in the mediæval period, the sense given it in Scripture. "Let not him that is deceived trust in Vanity, for Vanity shall be his recompense." "Vanity of Vanities." "The Lord knoweth the thoughts of the wise, that they are vain." It is difficult to find this sin,— which, after Pride, is the most universal, perhaps the most fatal, of all, fretting the whole depth of

our humanity into storm, "to waft a feather or
to drown a fly,"—definitely expressed in art.
Even Spenser, I think, has only partially expressed it under the figure of Phædria, more
properly Idle Mirth, in the second book. The
idea is, however, entirely worked out in the'
Vanity Fair of the 'Pilgrim's Progress.'

§ xcii. *Eighth side.* Envy. One of the
noblest pieces of expression in the series. She
is pointing malignantly with her finger; a serpent is wreathed about her head like a cap,
another forms the girdle of her waist, and a
dragon rests in her lap.

Giotto has, however, represented her, with
still greater subtlety, as having her fingers terminating in claws, and raising her right hand
with an expression partly of impotent regret,
partly of involuntary grasping; a serpent, issuing from her mouth, is about to bite her between
the eyes; she has long membranous ears, horns
on her head, and flames consuming her body.
The Envy of Spenser is only inferior to that of
Giotto, because the idea of folly and quickness of
hearing is not suggested by the size of the ear:
in other respects it is even finer, joining the idea
of fury, in the wolf on which he rides, with that
of corruption on his lips, and of discolouration or
distortion in the whole mind:

> " Malicious Envy rode
> Upon a ravenous wolfe, and still did chaw

Between his cankred teeth a venemous tode,
That all the poison ran about his jaw.
All in a kirtle of discoloured say
He clothed was, ypaynted full of eies,
And in his bosome secretly there lay
An hatefull snake, the which his taile uptyes
In many folds, and mortall sting implyes."

He has developed the idea in more detail, and still more loathsomely, in the twelfth canto of the fifth book.

§ XCIII. ELEVENTH CAPITAL. Its decoration is composed of eight birds, arranged as shown in Plate V. of the 'Seven Lamps,' which, however, was sketched from the Renaissance copy. These birds are all varied in form and action, but not so as to require special description.

§ XCIV. TWELFTH CAPITAL. This has been very·interesting, but is grievously defaced, four of its figures being entirely broken away, and the character of two others quite undecipherable. It is fortunate that it has been copied in the thirty-third capital of the Renaissance series, from which we are able to identify the lost figures.

First side. Misery. A man with a wan face, seemingly pleading with a child who has its hands crossed on its breast. There is a buckle at its own breast in the shape of a cloven heart. Inscribed " MISERIA."

The intention of this figure is not altogether

apparent, as it is by no means treated as a vice ;
the distress seeming real, and like that of a
parent in poverty mourning over his child.   Yet
it seems placed here as in direct opposition to
the virtue of Cheerfulness, which follows next
in order; rather, however, I believe, with the
intention of illustrating human life, than the
character of the vice, which, as we have seen,
Dante placed in the circle of hell.   The word in
that case would, I think, have been "Tristitia,"
the " unholy Griefe " of Spenser,—

> " All in sable sorrowfully clad,
> Downe hanging his dull head with heavy chere ;
> *   *   *   *   .   *   *
> A pair of pincers in his hand he had,
> With which he pinchèd people to the heart."

He has farther amplified the idea under another
figure in the fifth canto of the fourth book :

> " His name was Care ; a blacksmith by his trade,
> That neither day nor night from working spared ;
> But to small purpose yron wedges made :
> Those be unquiet thoughts that carefull minds invade.
> Rude was his garment, and to rags all rent,
> No better had he, ne for better cared :
> With blistered hands among the cinders brent."

It is to be noticed, however, that in the
Renaissance copy this figure is stated to be, not
Miseria, but "Misericordia."   The contraction is
a very moderate one, Misericordia being in old

MS. written always as "Mia." If this reading be right, the figure is placed here rather as the companion, than the opposite, of Cheerfulness; unless, indeed, it is intended to unite the idea of Mercy and compassion with that of Sacred Sorrow.

§ xcv. *Second side.* Cheerfulness. A woman with long flowing hair, crowned with roses, playing on a tambourine, and with open lips, as singing. Inscribed " ALACRITAS."

We have already met with this virtue among those especially set by Spenser to attend on Womanhood. It is inscribed in the Renaissance copy, "ALACHRITAS CHANIT MECUM." Note the gutturals of the rich and fully developed Venetian dialect now affecting the Latin, which is free from them in the earlier capitals.

§ xcvi. *Third side.* Destroyed ; but, from the copy, we find it has been Stultitia, Folly ; and it is there represented simply as a man *riding,* a sculpture worth the consideration of the English residents who bring their horses to Venice. Giotto gives Stultitia a feather cap, and club. In early manuscripts he is always eating with one hand, and striking with the other ; in later ones he has a cap and bells, or cap crested with a cock's head, whence the word " coxcomb."

§ xcvii. *Fourth side.* Destroyed, all but a book, which identifies it with the "Celestial

Chastity " of the Renaissance copy; there represented as a woman pointing to a book (connecting the convent life with the pursuit of literature ?).

Spenser's Chastity, Britomart, is the most exquisitely wrought of all his characters; but, as before noticed, she is not the Chastity of the convent, but of wedded life.

§ XCVIII. *Fifth side.* Only a scroll is left, but, from the copy, we find it has been Honesty or Truth. Inscribed "HONESTATEM DILIGO." It is very curious, that among all the Christian systems of the virtues which we have examined, we should find this one in Venice only.

The Truth of Spenser, Una, is, after Chastity, the most exquisite character in the " Faerie Queen."

§ XCIX. *Sixth side.* Falsehood. An old woman leaning on a crutch: and inscribed in the copy, "FALSITAS IN ME SEMPER EST." The Fidessa of Spenser, the great enemy of Una, or Truth, is far more subtly conceived, probably not without special reference to the Papal deceits. In her true form she is a loathsome hag, but in her outward aspect,

"A goodly lady, clad in scarlet red,
  Purfled with gold and pearle: * *
  Her wanton palfrey all was overspred
  With tinsell trappings, woven like a wave,
  Whose bridle rung with golden bels and bosses brave."

Dante's Fraud, Geryon, is the finest personification of all, but the description (Inferno, Canto XVII.) is too long to be quoted.

§ c. *Seventh side.* Injustice. An armed figure holding a halbert; so also in the copy. The figure used by Giotto with the particular intention of representing unjust government, is represented at the gate of an embattled castle in a forest, between rocks, while various deeds of violence are committed at his feet. Spenser's "Adicia" is a furious hag, at last transformed into a tiger.

Eighth side. A man with a dagger looking sorrowfully at a child, who turns his back to him. I cannot understand this figure. It is inscribed in the copy, "ASTINECIA (Abstinentia?) OPITIMA?"

§ CI. THIRTEENTH CAPITAL. It has lions' heads all round, coarsely cut.

FOURTEENTH CAPITAL. It has various animals, each sitting on its haunches. Three dogs, one a greyhound, one long-haired, one short-haired with bells about its neck, two monkeys, one with fan-shaped hair projecting on each side of its face; a noble boar, with its tusks, hoofs, and bristles sharply cut ; and a lion and lioness.

§ CII. FIFTEENTH CAPITAL. The pillar to which it belongs is thicker than the rest, as well as the one over it in the upper arcade.

The sculpture of this capital is also much coarser, and seems to me later than that of the

rest ; and it has no inscription, which is embarrass-
ing, as its subjects have had much meaning ; but
I believe Selvatico is right in supposing it to
have been intended for a general illustration of
Idleness.

First side. A woman with a distaff ; her girdle
richly decorated, and fastened by a buckle.

Second side. A youth in a long mantle, with
a rose in his hand.

Third side. A woman in a turban stroking a
puppy, which she holds by the haunches.

Fourth side. A man with a parrot.

Fifth side. A woman in very rich costume,
with braided hair, and dress thrown into minute
folds, holding a rosary (?) in her left hand, her
right on her breast.

Sixth side. A man with a very thoughtful face
laying his hand upon the leaves of the capital.

Seventh side. A crowned lady, with a rose in
her hand.

Eighth side. A boy with a ball in his left
hand, and his right laid on his breast.

§ CIII. SIXTEENTH CAPITAL. It is decorated
with eight large heads, partly intended to be
grotesque,* and very course and bad, except only

---

* Selvatico states that these are intended to be representative of eight nations—Latins, Tartars, Turks, Hungarians,
Greeks, Goths, Egyptians, and Persians. Either the inscriptions are now defaced, or I have carelessly omitted to note
them.

that in the sixth side, which is totally different from all the rest, and looks like a portrait. It is thin, thoughtful, and dignified; thoroughly fine in every way. It wears a cap surmounted by two winged lions; and, therefore, I think Selvatico must have inaccurately written the list given in the note, for this head is certainly meant to express the superiority of the Venetian character over that of other nations. Nothing is more remarkable in all early sculpture than its appreciation of the signs of dignity of character in the features, and the way in which it can exalt the principal figure in any subject by a few touches.

§ CIV. SEVENTEENTH CAPITAL. This has been so destroyed by the sea wind, which creeps at this point of the arcade round the angle of the palace, that its inscriptions are no longer legible, and great part of its figures are gone. Selvatico states them as follows: Solomon, the wise; Priscian, the grammarian; Aristotle, the logician; Tully, the orator; Pythagoras, the philosopher; Archimedes, the mechanic; Orpheus, the musician; Ptolemy, the astronomer. The fragments actually remaining are the following:

First side. A figure with two books, in a robe richly decorated with circles of roses. Inscribed " SALOMON (SAP)IENS."

Second side. A man with one book, poring over it: he has had a long stick or reed in his hand. Of inscription only the letters "GRAM-MATIC" remain.

Third side. "ARISTOTLE"; so inscribed. He has a peaked double beard and a flat cap, from under which his long hair falls down his back.

Fourth side. Destroyed.

Fifth side. Destroyed, all but a board with three (counters ?) on it.

Sixth side. A figure with compasses. In-scribed " GEOMET * *."

Seventh side. Nothing is left but a guitar with its handle wrought into a lion's head.

Eighth side. Destroyed.

§ CV. We have now arrived at the EIGHT-EENTH CAPITAL, the most interesting and beau-tiful of the palace. It represents the planets, and the sun and moon, in those divisions of the zodiac known to astrologers as their " houses "; and perhaps indicates, by the position in which they are placed, the period of the year at which this great corner-stone was laid. The inscriptions above have been in quaint Latin rhyme, but are now decipherable only in frag-ments, and that with the more difficulty because the rusty iron bar that binds the abacus has broken away, in its expansion, nearly all the upper portions of the stone, and with them the signs of contraction, which are of great import-ance. I shall give the fragments of them that I could decipher ; first, as the letters actually stand (putting those of which I am doubtful in brackets, with a note of interrogation), and then as I would read them.

§ CVI. It should be premised that, in modern astrology, the houses of the planets are thus arranged :

The house of the Sun   is Leo.
  ,,   ,, Moon   ,, Cancer.
  ,,   of Mars   ,, Aries and Scorpio.
  ,,   ,, Venus   ,, Taurus and Libra.
  ,,   ,, Mercury ,, Gemini and Virgo.
  ,,   ,, Jupiter   ,, Sagittarius and
                                   Pisces.
  ,,   ,, Saturn   ,, Capricorn.
  ,,   ,, Herschel ,, Aquarius.

The Herschel planet being of course unknown to the old astrologers, we have only the other six planetary powers, together with the sun; and Aquarius is assigned to Saturn as his house. I could not find Capricorn at all; but this sign may have been broken away, as the whole capital is grievously defaced. The eighth side of the capital, which the Herschel planet would now have occupied, bears a sculpture of the Creation of Man: it is the most conspicuous side, the one set diagonally across the angle; or the eighth in our usual mode of reading the capitals, from which I shall not depart.

§ CVII. The *first side*, then, or that towards the Sea, has Aquarius as the house of Saturn, represented as a seated figure beautifully draped, pouring a stream of water out of an amphora over the leaves of the capital.   His inscription is:

"ET SATURNE DOMUS (ECLOCERUNT?) 1ˢ 7BRE."

§ CVIII. *Second side.*   Jupiter, in his houses Sagittarius and Pisces, represented throned, with an upper dress disposed in radiating folds about his neck, and hanging down upon his breast, ornamented by small pendent trefoiled studs or bosses.   He wears the drooping bonnet and long gloves; but the folds about the neck, shot forth to express the rays of the star, are the most remarkable characteristic of the figure.   He raises his sceptre in his left hand over Sagittarius, represented as the centaur Chiron; and holds two thunnies in his right.   Something rough, like a third fish, has been broken away below them; the more easily because this part of the group is entirely undercut, and the two fish glitter in the light, relieved on the deep gloom below the leaves. The inscription is:

'INDE JOVI' * DONA PISES SIMUL ATQ' CIRONA."

* The comma in these inscriptions stands for a small cuneiform mark, I believe of contraction, and the small * for a zigzag mark of the same kind. The dots or periods are similarly marked on the stone.

Or,

> " Inde Jovis dona
> Pisces simul atque Chirona."

Domus is, I suppose, to be understood before Jovis: "Then the house of Jupiter gives (or governs?) the fishes and Chiron."

§ CIX. *Third side.* Mars, in his houses Aries and Scorpio. Represented as a very ugly knight in chain mail, seated sideways on the ram, whose horns are broken away, and having a large scorpion in his left hand, whose tail is broken also, to the infinite injury of the group, for it seems to have curled across to the angle leaf, and formed a bright line of light, like the fish in the hand of Jupiter. The knight carries a shield, on which fire and water are sculptured, and bears a banner upon his lance, with the word "DEFE-ROSUM," which puzzled me for some time. It should be read, I believe, " De ferro sum," which would be good *Venetian* Latin for "I am of iron."

§ CX. *Fourth side.* The sun, in his house Leo. Represented under the figure of Apollo, sitting on the lion, with rays shooting from his head, and the world in his hand. The inscription :

" TU ES DOMU' SOLIS (QUO* ?) SIGNE LEONI."

I believe the first phrase is, "Tunc est Domus

solis ; " but there is a letter gone after the " quo,"
and I have no idea what case of signum " signe "
stands for.

§ cxi. *Fifth side.* Venus, in her houses
Taurus and Libra. The most beautiful figure of
the series. She sits upon the bull, who is deep
in the dewlap, and better cut than most of the
animals, holding a mirror in her right hand, and
the scales in her left. Her breast is very nobly
and tenderly indicated under the folds of her
drapery, which is exquisitely studied in its fall.
What is left of the inscription runs

"LIBRA CUM TAURO DOMUS * * * PURIOR AUR*."

§ cxii. *Sixth side.* Mercury, represented as
wearing a pendent cap, and holding a book : he
is supported by three children in reclining attitudes, representing his houses Gemini and Virgo.
But I cannot understand the inscription, though
more than usually legible :

"OCCUPAT ERIGONE STIBONS GEMINUQ' LACONE."

§ cxiii. *Seventh side.* The Moon, in her house
Cancer. This sculpture, which is turned towards
the Piazzetta, is the most picturesque of the series.
The moon is represented as a woman in a boat
upon the sea, who raises the crescent in her right
hand, and with her left draws a crab out of the
waves, up the boat's side. The moon was, I

believe, represented in Egyptian sculptures as
in a boat; but I rather think the Venetian was
not aware of this, and that he meant to express
the peculiar sweetness of the moonlight at Venice,
as seen across the lagoons. Whether this was
intended by putting the planet in the boat, may
be questionable, but assuredly the idea was meant
to be conveyed by the dress of the figure. For
all the draperies of the other figures on this
capital, as well as on the rest of the façade, are
disposed in severe but full folds, showing little of
the forms beneath them; but the moon's drapery
ripples down to her feet, so as exactly to suggest
the trembling of the moonlight on the waves.
This beautiful idea is highly characteristic of
the thoughtfulness of the early sculptures: five
hundred men may be now found who could have
cut the drapery, as such, far better, for one who
would have disposed its folds with this intention.
The inscription is:

"LUNE CANCER DOMU T. PBET IORBE SIGNORU."

§ CXIV. *Eighth side.* God creating man. Represented as a throned figure, with a glory round the
head, laying his left hand on the head of a naked
youth, and sustaining him with his right hand.
The inscription puzzled me for a long time; but
except the lost r and m of "formavit," and a letter
quite undefaced. but to me unintelligible, before

the word Eva, in the shape of a figure of 7, I
have safely ascertained the rest :

"DELIMO DSADA DECO STAFO * * AVIT7EVA."

Or

" De limo Dominus Adam, de costa fo(rm)avit Evam ; "

From the dust the Lord made Adam, and from the rib Eve.

I imagine the whole of this capital, therefore—
the principal one of the old palace,—to have been
intended to signify, first, the formation of the
planets for the service of man upon the earth ;
secondly, the entire subjection of the fates and
fortune of man to the will of God, as determined
from the time when the earth and stars were
made, and, in fact, written in the volume of the
stars themselves.

Thus interpreted, the doctrines of judicial
astrology were not only consistent with, but
an aid to, the most spiritual and humble
Christianity.

In the workmanship and grouping of its
foliage, this capital is, on the whole, the finest
I know in Europe. The sculptor has put his
whole strength into it. I trust that it will
appear among the other Venetian casts lately
taken for the Crystal Palace ; but if not, I have
myself cast all its figures, and two of its leaves,
and I intend to give drawings of them on a large
scale in my folio work.

§ CXV. NINETEENTH CAPITAL. This is, of course, the second counting from the Sea, on ·the Piazzetta side of the palace, calling that of the Fig-tree angle the first.

It is the most important capital, as a piece of evidence in point of dates, in the whole palace. Great pains have been taken with it, and in some portion of the accompanying furniture or ornaments of each of its figures a small piece of coloured marble has been inlaid, with peculiar significance; for the capital represents the *arts of sculpture and architecture;* and the inlaying of the coloured stones (which are far too small to be effective at a distance, and are found in this one capital only of the whole series) is merely an expression of the architect's feeling of the essential importance of this art of inlaying, and of the value of colour generally in his own art.

§ CXVI. *First side.* "ST. SIMPLICIUS": so inscribed. A figure working with a pointed chisel on a small oblong block of green serpentine, about four inches long by one wide, inlaid in the capital. The chisel is, of course, in the left hand, but the right is held up open, with the palm outwards.

Second side. A crowned figure, carving the image of a child on a small statue, with a ground of red marble. The sculptured figure is highly finished, and is in type of head much like the Ham or Japheth at the Vine angle. Inscription effaced.

Third side. An old man, uncrowned, but with curling hair, at work on a small column, with its capital complete, and a little shaft of dark red marble, spotted with paler red. The capital is precisely of the form of that found in the palace of the Tiepolos and the other thirteenth century work of Venice. This one figure would be quite enough, without any other evidence whatever, to determine the date of this flank of the Ducal Palace as not later, at all events, than the first half of the fourteenth century. Its inscription is broken away, all but " DISIPULO."

Fourth side. A crowned figure; but the object on which it has been working is broken away, and all the inscription except " ST. E(N ?)AS."

Fifth side. A man with a turban and a sharp chisel, at work on a kind of panel or niche, the back of which is of red marble.

Sixth side. A crowned figure, with hammer and chisel, employed *on a little range of windows of the fifth order*, having roses set, instead of orbicular ornaments, between the spandrils, with a rich cornice, and a band of purple marble inserted above. This sculpture assures us of the date of the fifth order window, which it shows to have been universal in the early fourteenth century.

There are also five arches in the block on which the sculptor is working, marking the frequency of the number five in the window groups of the time.

Seventh side. A figure at work on a pilaster, with Lombardic thirteenth century capital (for account of the series of forms in Venetian capitals see the final Appendix of the next volume), the shaft of dark red spotted marble.

Eighth side. A figure with a rich open crown, working on a delicate recumbent statue, the head of which is laid on a pillow covered with a rich chequer pattern ; the whole supported on a block of dark red marble. Inscription broken away, all but " ST. SYM (Symmachus ?) TV * * ANVS." There appear, therefore, altogether to have been five saints, two of them popes, if Simplicius is the pope of that name (three in front, two on the fourth and sixth sides), alternating with the three uncrowned workmen in the manual labour of sculpture. I did not, therefore, insult our present architects in saying above * that they "ought to work in the mason's yard with their men." It would be difficult to find a more interesting expression of the devotional spirit in which all great work was undertaken at this time.

§ CXVII. TWENTIETH CAPITAL. Adorned with heads of animals, and so simply characteristic, indeed, of the grandeur of style in the entire building, that I chose it for the first plate in my folio work. In spite of the sternness of its plan,

* The reference is to a passage in the old edition, unnecessary here, but which cannot be too strongly reiterated, in its proper place.

however, it is wrought with great care in surface detail; and the ornamental value of the minute chasing obtained by the delicate plumage of the birds, and the clustered bees on the honeycomb in the bear's mouth, opposed to the strong simplicity of its general form, cannot be too much admired. There are also more grace, life, and variety in the sprays of foliage on each side of it, and under the heads, than in any other capital of the series, though the earliness of the workmanship is marked by considerable hardness and coldness in the larger heads. A Northern Gothic workman, better acquainted with bears and wolves than it was possible to become in St. Mark's Place, would have put far more life into these heads, but he could not have composed them more skilfully.

§ CXVIII. *First side.* A lion with a stag's haunch in his mouth. Those readers who have the folio plate, should observe the peculiar way in which the ear is cut into the shape of a ring, jagged or furrowed on the edge; an archaic mode of treatment peculiar, in the Ducal Palace, to the lions' heads of the fourteenth century. The moment we reach the Renaissance work, the lions' ears are smooth. Inscribed simply, " LEO."

Second side. A wolf with a dead bird in his mouth, its body wonderfully true in expression of the passiveness of death. The feathers are each wrought with a central quill and radiating filaments. Inscribed " LUPUS."

Third side. A fox, not at all like one, with a dead cock in his mouth, its comb and pendent neck admirably designed so as to fall across the great angle leaf of the capital, its tail hanging down on the other side, its long straight feathers exquisitely cut. Inscribed "(VULP ?)IS."

Fourth side. Entirely broken away.

Fifth side. "APER." Well tusked, with a head of maize in his mouth; at least I suppose it to be maize, though shaped like a pine-cone.

Sixth side. "CHANIS." With a bone, very ill cut; and a bald-headed species of dog, with ugly flap ears.

Seventh side. "MUSCIPULUS." With a rat (?) in his mouth.

Eighth side. "URSUS." With a honeycomb, covered with large bees.

§ CXIX. TWENTY-FIRST CAPITAL. Represents the principal inferior professions.

First side. An old man, with his brow deeply wrinkled, and very expressive features, beating in a kind of mortar with a hammer. Inscribed " LAPICIDA SUM."

Second side. I believe, a goldsmith; he is striking a small flat bowl or patera, on a pointed anvil, with a light hammer. The inscription is gone.

Third side. A shoemaker, with a shoe in his hand, and an instrument for cutting leather suspended beside him. Inscription undecipherable.

Fourth side. Much broken. A carpenter planing a beam resting on two horizontal logs. Inscribed " CARPENTARIUS SUM."

Fifth side. A figure shovelling fruit into a tub; the latter very carefully carved from what appears to have been an excellent piece of cooperage. Two thin laths cross each other over the top of it. The inscription, now lost, was, according to Selvatico, " MENSURATOR "?

Sixth side. A man, with a large hoe, breaking the ground, which lies in irregular furrows and clods before him. Now undecipherable, but, according to Selvatico, " ACRICHOLA."

Seventh side. A man, in a pendent cap, writing on a large scroll which falls over his knee. Inscribed " NOTARIUS SUM."

Eighth side. A smith forging a sword or scythe-blade; he wears a large skull-cap; beats with a large hammer on a solid anvil; and is inscribed " FABER SUM."

§ CXX. TWENTY-SECOND CAPITAL. The Ages of Man; and the influence of the planets on human life.

First side. The moon, governing infancy for four years, according to Selvatico. I have no note of this side, having, I suppose, been prevented from raising the ladder against it by some fruit-stall or other impediment in the regular course of my examination; and then forgotten to return to it.

Second side. A child with a tablet, and an alphabet inscribed on it. The legend above is

"MĒCUBEU' DNT̄. PUEBICIE. PAṄ. X̣."

Or, " Mercurius dominatur pueritæ per annos X."
(Selvatico reads VII.) "Mercury governs boy-hood for ten (or seven) years."

Third side. An older youth, with another tablet, but broken. Inscribed

"ADOLOSCENCIE * * * P. AN. VII."

Selvatico misses this side altogether, as I did the first, so that the lost planet is irrecoverable, as the inscription is now defaced. Note the o for e in adolescentia ; so also we constantly find u for o ; showing, together with much other incontestable evidence of the same kind, how full and deep the old pronunciation of Latin always remained, and how ridiculous our English mincing of the vowels would have sounded to a Roman ear.

Fourth side. A youth with a hawk on his fist.

"IUVENTUTI D̄NT̄ SOL. P. AN. XIX."
The sun governs youth for nineteen years.

Fifth side. A man sitting, helmed, with a sword over his shoulder. Inscribed

"SENECTUTI D̄NT̄ MABS. P. AN. XV."
Mars governs manhood for fifteen years.

Sixth side. A very graceful and serene figure, in the pendent cap, reading.

"SENICIE DNT̂ JUPITER, P. ANN. XII."
Jupiter governs age for twelve years.

Seventh side. An old man in a skull-cap, praying.

"DECREPITE D̂N̂T̂ SATN̂ UQ⁹ ADMŌTĒ." (Saturnus usque ad mortem.)
Saturn governs decrepitude until death.

Eighth side. The dead body lying on a mattress.

"ULTIMA EST MORS PENA PECCATI."
Last comes death, the penalty of sin.

§ CXXI. Shakespeare's Seven Ages are of course merely the expression of this early and well-known system. He has deprived the dotage of its devotion; but I think wisely, as the Italian system would imply that devotion was, or should be, always delayed until dotage.

TWENTY-THIRD CAPITAL. I agree with Selvatico in thinking this has been restored. It is decorated with large and vulgar heads.

§ CXXII. TWENTY-FOURTH CAPITAL. This belongs to the large shaft which sustains the great party wall of the Sala del Gran Consiglio. The shaft is thicker than the rest; but the capital, though ancient, is coarse and somewhat inferior

in design to the others of the series. It represents the history of marriage : the lover first
seeing his mistress at a window, then addressing
her, bringing her presents ; then the bridal, the
birth and the death of a child. But I have not
been able to examine these sculptures properly,
because the pillar is encumbered by the railing
which surrounds the two guns set before the
Austrian guard-house.

§ CXXIII. TWENTY-FIFTH CAPITAL. We have
here the employments of the months, with which
we are already tolerably acquainted. There are,
however, one or two varieties worth noticing in
this series.

First side. March. Sitting triumphantly in
a rich dress, as the beginning of the year.

Second side. April and May. April with a
lamb : May with a feather fan in her hand.

Third side. June. Carrying cherries in a
basket.

I did not give this series with the others in
the previous chapter, because this representation
of June is peculiarly Venetian. It is called " the
month of cherries," mese delle ceriese, in the
popular rhyme on the conspiracy of Tiepolo.

The cherries principally grown near Venice
are of a deep red colour, and large, but not of
high flavour, though refreshing. They are
carved upon the pillar with great care, all
their stalks undercut.

Fourth side. July and August. The first reaping; the *leaves* of the straw being given, shooting out from the tubular stalk. August, opposite, beats (the grain?) in a basket.

Fifth side. September. A woman standing in a wine-tub, and holding a branch of vine. Very beautiful.

Sixth side. October and November. I could not make out their occupation; they seem to be roasting or boiling some root over a fire.

Seventh side. December. Killing pigs, as usual.

Eighth side. January warming his feet, and February frying fish. This last employment is again as characteristic of the Venetian winter as the cherries are of the Venetian summer.

The inscriptions are undecipherable, except a few letters here and there, and the words MARCIUS, APRILIS, and FEBRUARIUS.

This is the last of the capitals of the early palace; the next, or twenty-sixth capital, is the first of those executed in the fifteenth century under Foscari; and hence to the Judgment angle the traveller has nothing to do but to compare the base copies of the earlier work with their originals, or to observe the total want of invention in the Renaissance sculptor, wherever he has depended on his own resources. This, however, always with the exception of the twenty-seventh and of the last capital, which are both fine.

I shall merely enumerate the subjects and point out the plagiarisms of these capitals, as they are not worth description.

§ CXXIV. TWENTY-SIXTH CAPITAL. Copied from the fifteenth, merely changing the succession of the figures.

TWENTY-SEVENTH CAPITAL. I think it possible that this may be part of the old work displaced in joining the new palace with the old: at all events, it is well designed, though a little coarse. It represents eight different kinds of fruit, each in a basket; the characters well given, and groups well arranged, but without much care or finish. The names are inscribed above, though somewhat unnecessarily, and with certainly as much disrespect to the beholder's intelligence as the sculptor's art—namely, ZEREXIS, PIRI, CHUCUMERIS, PERSICI, ZUCHE, MOLONI, FICI, HUVA. Zerexis (cherries) and Zuche (gourds) both begin with the same letter, whether meant for z, s, or c, I am not sure. The Zuche are the common gourds, divided into two protuberances, one larger than the other, like a bottle compressed near the neck; and the Moloni are the long water-melons, which, roasted, form a staple food of the Venetians to this day.

§ CXXV. TWENTY-EIGHTH CAPITAL. Copied from the seventh.

TWENTY-NINTH CAPITAL. Copied from the ninth.

THIRTIETH CAPITAL. Copied from the tenth. The "Accidia" is noticeable as having the inscription complete, "ACCIDIA ME STRINGIT;" and the "Luxuria" for its utter want of expression, having a severe and calm face, a robe up to the neck, and her hand upon her breast. The inscription is also different: "LUXURIA SUM STERC, (?) INFERI (?)."

THIRTY-FIRST CAPITAL. Copied from the eighth.

THIRTY-SECOND CAPITAL. Has no inscription, only fully robed figures laying their hands, without any meaning, on their own shoulders heads, or chins, or on the leaves around them.

THIRTY-THIRD CAPITAL. Copied from the twelfth.

THIRTY-FOURTH CAPITAL. Copied from the eleventh.

THIRTY-FIFTH CAPITAL. Has children, with birds or fruit, pretty in features, and utterly inexpressive, like the cherubs of the eighteenth century.

§ CXXVI. THIRTY-SIXTH CAPITAL. This is the last of the Piazzetta façade, the elaborate one under the Judgment angle. Its foliage is copied from the eighteenth at the opposite side, with an endeavour on the part of the Renaissance sculptor to refine upon it, by which he has merely lost some of its truth and force. This capital will, however, be always thought, at first, the most

beautiful of the whole series : and indeed it is
very noble; its groups of figures most carefully
studied, very graceful, and much more pleasing
than those of the earlier work, though with less
real power in them ; and its foliage is only inferior to that of the magnificent Fig-tree angle.
It represents, on its front or first side, Justice
enthroned, seated on two lions; and on the
seven other sides examples of acts of justice
or good government, or figures of lawgivers, in
the following order :

Second side. Aristotle, with two pupils, giving
laws. Inscribed

"ARISTOT * * CHE DIE LEGE."

Aristotle, who declares laws.

Third side. I have mislaid my note of this
side : Selvatico and Lazari call it " Isidore " (?) *

Fourth side. Solon with his pupils. Inscribed

"SAL° UNO DEI SETE SAVI DI GRECIA CHE DIE LEGE."

Solon, one of the seven sages of Greece, who declares laws.

Note, by-the-bye, the pure Venetian dialect used
in this capital, instead of the Latin in the more
ancient ones. One of the seated pupils in this

* Can they have mistaken the ISIPIONE of the fifth side for
the word Isidore ?

sculpture is remarkably beautiful in the sweep of his flowing drapery.

Fifth side. The chastity of Scipio. Inscribed

"ISIPIONE A CHASTITA CH * * * E LA FIA (e la figlia?)
* * ARE."

A soldier in a plumed bonnet presents a kneeling maiden to the seated Scipio, who turns thoughtfully away.

Sixth side. Numa Pompilius building churches.

"NUMA POMPILIO IMPERADOR EDIFICHADOR DI TEMPI
E CHIESE."

Numa, in a kind of hat with a crown above it, directing a soldier in Roman armour (note this as contrasted with the mail of the earlier capitals). They point to a tower of three stories filled with tracery.

Seventh side. Moses receiving the law. Inscribed

"QUANDO MOSE RECEVE LA LEGE I SUL MONTE."

Moses kneels on a rock, whence springs a beautifully fancied tree, with clusters of three berries in the centre of three leaves, sharp and quaint, like fine Northern Gothic. The half figure of the Deity comes out of the abacus, the arm meeting that of Moses, both at full stretch, with the stone tablets between.

Eighth side. Trajan doing justice to the Widow.

"TRAJANO IMPERADOR CHE FA JUSTITIA A LA VEDOVA."

He is riding spiritedly, his mantle blown out behind: the widow kneeling before his horse.

§ CXXVII. The reader will observe that this capital is of peculiar interest in its relation to the much-disputed question of the character of the later government of Venice. It is the assertion by that government of its belief that Justice only could be the foundation of its stability, as these stones of Justice and Judgment are the foundation of its halls of council. And this profession of their faith may be interpreted in two ways. Most modern historians would call it, in common with the continual reference to the principles of justice in the political and judicial language of the period,* nothing more than a cloak for consummate violence and guilt; and it may easily be proved to have been so in myriads of instances. But in the main, I believe the expression of feeling to be genuine.

---

* Compare the speech of the Doge Mocenigo, above— " first justice, and *then* the interests of the state :" and see (in the old edition) Vol. III. Chap. II. § LIX.,

I do not believe, of the majority of the leading
Venetians of this period whose portraits have
come down to us, that they were deliberately
and everlastingly hypocrites.   I see no hypocrisy in their countenances.   Much capacity of
it, much subtlety, much natural and acquired
reserve; but no meanness.   On the contrary,
infinite grandeur, repose, courage, and the peculiar unity and tranquillity of expression which
come of sincerity or *wholeness* of heart, and which
it would take much demonstration to make me
believe could by any possibility be seen on the
countenance of an insincere man.   I trust,
therefore, that these Venetian nobles of the
fifteenth century did, in the main, desire to do
judgment and justice to all men ; but, as the
whole system of morality had been by this time
undermined by the teaching of the Romish
Church, the idea of justice had become separated from that of truth, so that dissimulation
in the interest of the state assumed the aspect
of duty.   We had, perhaps, better consider,
with some carefulness, the mode in which our
own government is carried on, and the occasional difference between parliamentary and
private ·morality, before we judge mercilessly
of the Venetians in this respect.   The secrecy
with which their political and criminal trials
were conducted, appears to modern eyes like a
confession of sinister intentions ; but may it

not also be considered, and with more probability, as the result of an endeavour to do justice
in an age of violence?—the only means by
which Law could establish its footing in the
midst of feudalism. Might not Irish juries at
this day justifiably desire to conduct their proceedings with some greater approximation to
the judicial principles of the Council of Ten?
Finally, if we examine, with critical accuracy,
the evidence on which our present impressions
of Venetian government are founded, we shall
discover, in the first place, that two-thirds of
the traditions of its cruelties are romantic
fables: in the second, that the crimes of which
it can be proved to have been guilty differ only
from those committed by the other Italian
powers in being done less wantonly, and under
profounder conviction of their political expediency: and, lastly, that the final degradation of
the Venetian power appears owing not so much
to the principles of its government, as to their
being forgotten in the pursuit of pleasure.

§ CXXVIII. We have now examined the portions
of the palace which contain the principal
evidence of the feeling of its builders. The
capitals of the upper arcade are exceedingly
various in their character; their design is formed,
as in the lower series, of eight leaves, thrown into
volutes at the angles, and sustaining figures at
the flanks; but these figures have no inscriptions,

and though evidently not without meaning, cannot be interpreted without more knowledge than
I possess of ancient symbolism. Many of the
capitals towards the sea appear to have been
restored, and to be rude copies of the ancient
ones ; others, though apparently original, have
been somewhat carelessly wrought; but those
of them which are both genuine and carefully
treated are even finer in composition than any,
except the eighteenth, in the lower arcade. The
traveller in Venice ought to ascend into the cor-
ridor, and examine with great care the series of
capitals which extend on the Piazzetta side from
the fig-tree angle to the pilaster which carries
the party wall of the Sala del Gran Consiglio.
As examples of graceful composition in massy
capitals meant for hard service and distant effect,
these are among the finest things I know in
Gothic art; and that above the fig-tree is remarkable for its sculptures of the four winds ;
each on the side turned towards the wind represented. Levante, the east wind ; a figure with
rays round its head, to show that it is always
clear weather when that wind blows, raising
the sun out of the sea : Hotro, the south wind ;
crowned ; holding the sun in its right hand :
Ponente, the west wind ; plunging the sun into
the sea : and Tramontana, the north wind ; looking up at the north star. This capital should
be carefully examined, if for no other reason

than to attach greater distinctness of idea to the magnificent verbiage of Milton:—

> "Thwart of these, as fierce,
> Forth rush the Levant and the Ponent winds,
> Eurus, and Zephyr; with their lateral noise,
> Sirocco, and Libecchio."

I may also especially point out the bird feeding its three young ones on the seventh pillar on the Piazzetta side; but there is no end to the fantasy of these sculptures; and the traveller ought to observe them all carefully, until he comes to the great pilaster or complicated pier which sustains the party wall of the Sala del Consiglio; that is to say, the forty-seventh capital of the whole series, counting from the pilaster of the Vine angle inclusive, as in the series of the lower arcade. The forty-eighth, forty-ninth, and fiftieth are bad work, but they are old; the fifty-first is the first Renaissance capital of the upper arcade; the first new lion's head with smooth ears, cut in the time of Foscari, is over the fiftieth capital; and that capital, with its shaft, stands on the apex of the eighth arch from the sea on the Piazzetta side, of which one spandril is masonry of the fourteenth, and the other of the fifteenth, century.

§ CXXIX. The reader who is not able to examine the building on the spot may be surprised at the definiteness with which the point of junction is ascertainable; but a glance at the lowest range of leaves in the opposite Plate (XX.: see note at end of volume), will enable him to judge of the grounds on which the above statement is made. Fig. 12 is a cluster of leaves from the capital of the Four Winds; early work of the finest time. Fig. 13 is a leaf from the great Renaissance capital at the Judgment angle, worked in imitation of the older leafage. Fig. 14 is a leaf from one of the Renaissance capitals of the upper arcade, which were all worked in the natural manner of the period. It will be seen that it requires no great ingenuity to distinguish between such design as that of Fig. 12 and that of Fig. 14.

§ CXXX. It is very possible that the reader may at first like Fig. 14 the best. I shall endeavour, in the next chapter, to show why he should not; but it must also be noted, that Fig. 12 has lost, and Fig. 14 gained, both largely, under the hands of the engraver. All the bluntness and coarseness of feeling in the workmanship of Fig. 14 have disappeared on this small scale, and all the subtle refinements in the broad masses of Fig. 12 have vanished. They could not, indeed, be rendered in line engraving, unless by the hand of Albert Durer; and I have, therefore, abandoned, for the present, all endeavour to represent any more important mass of the early sculpture of the Ducal Palace : but I trust that, in a few months, casts of many portions will be within the reach of the inhabitants of London, and that they will be able to judge for themselves of their perfect, pure, unlaboured naturalism ; the freshness, elasticity, and softness of their leafage, united with the most noble symmetry and severe reserve,—no running to waste, no loose or experimental lines, no extravagance, and no weakness. Their design is always sternly architectural; there is none of the wildness or redundance of natural vegetation, but there is all the strength, freedom, and tossing flow of the breathing leaves, and all the undulation of their surfaces, rippled, as they grew, by the summer winds, as the sands are by the sea.

§ CXXXI. This early sculpture of the Ducal Palace, then, represents the state of Gothic work in Venice at its central and proudest period, *i.e.*, circa 1350. After this time, all is decline,—of what nature and by what steps, we shall inquire in the ensuing chapter ; for as this investigation, though still referring to Gothic architecture, introduces us to the first symptoms of the Renaissance influence, I have considered it as properly belonging to the third division of our subject.

§ CXXXII. And as, under the shadow of these nodding leaves, we bid farewell to the great Gothic spirit, here also we may cease our examination of the details of the Ducal Palace ; for above its upper arcade there are only the four traceried

windows,* and one or two of the third order on
the Rio Façade, which can be depended upon as
exhibiting the original workmanship of the older
palace. I examined the capitals of the four
other windows on the façade, and of those on the
Piazzetta, one by one, with great care, and I
found them all to be of far inferior workmanship
to those which retain their traceries : I believe
the stone framework of these windows must have
been so cracked and injured by the flames of the
great fire, as to render it necessary to replace it
by new traceries ; and that the present mouldings and capitals are base imitations of the
original ones.   The traceries were at first, however, restored in their complete form, as the
holes for the bolts which fasten the bases of
their shafts are still to be seen in the window-
sills, as well as the marks of the inner mouldings
on the soffits.   How much the stone facing of
the façade, the parapets, and the shafts and
niches of the angles, retain of their original
masonry, it is also impossible to determine ; but
there is nothing in the workmanship of any of
them demanding especial notice ; still less in the
large central windows on each façade, which are

---

* Some further details respecting these portions, as well as
some necessary confirmations of my statements of dates, are,
however, given in Appendix 1, Vol. III. (old edition). I
feared wearying the general reader by introducing them into
the text.

entirely of Renaissance execution. All that is
admirable in these portions of the building is the
disposition of their various parts and masses,
which is without doubt the same as in the
original fabric, and calculated, when seen from
a distance, to produce the same impression.

§ cxxxiii. Not so in the interior. All vestige
of the earlier modes of decoration was here, of
course, destroyed by the fires; and the severe
and religious work of Guariento and Bellini has
been replaced by the wildness of Tintoret and
the luxury of Veronese. But in this case, though
widely different in temper, the art of the renewal
was at least intellectually as great as that which
had perished; and though the halls of the Ducal
Palace are no more representative of the character of the men by whom it was built, each
of them is still a colossal casket of priceless
treasure; a treasure whose safety has till now
depended on its being despised, and which at
this moment, and as I write, is piece by piece
being destroyed for ever.

§ cxxxiv. The reader will forgive my quitting
our more immediate subject, in order briefly to
explain the causes and the nature of this destruction; for the matter is simply the most important
of all that can be brought under our present consideration respecting the state of art in Europe.

The fact is, that the greater number of persons
or societies throughout Europe, whom wealth, or

chance, or inheritance has put in possession of
valuable pictures, do not know a good picture
from a bad one,* and have no idea in what the
value of a picture really consists. The reputation of certain works is raised, partly by accident,
partly by the just testimony of artists, partly by
the various and generally bad taste of the public
(no picture, that I know of, has ever, in modern
times, attained popularity, in the full sense of
the term, without having some exceedingly bad
qualities mingled with its good ones), and when
this reputation has once been completely established, it little matters to what state the picture
may be reduced : few minds are so completely
devoid of imagination as to be unable to invest
it with the beauties which they have heard
attributed to it.

§ CXXXV. This being so, the pictures that are
most valued are for the most part those by
masters of established renown, which are highly
or neatly finished, and of a size small enough to
admit of their being placed in galleries or saloons,
so as to be made subjects of ostentation, and to
be easily seen by a crowd. For the support of

---

* Many persons, capable of quickly sympathising with any
excellence, when once pointed out to them, easily deceive
themselves into the supposition that they are judges of art.
There is only one real test of such power of judgment. Can
they, at a glance, discover a good picture obscured by the
filth, and confused among the rubbish, of the pawnbroker's or
dealer's garret?

the fame and value of such pictures, little more
is necessary than that they should be kept bright,
partly by cleaning, which is incipient destruction,
and partly by what is called "restoring," that is,
painting over, which is of course total destruction.
Nearly all the gallery pictures in modern Europe
have been more or less destroyed by one or other
of these operations, generally exactly in proportion to the estimation in which they are held;
and as, originally, the smaller and more highly
finished works of any great master are usually
his worst, the contents of many of our most
celebrated galleries are by this time, in reality,
of very small value indeed.

§ CXXXVI. On the other hand, the most precious
works of any noble painter are usually those
which have been done quickly, and in the heat
of the first thought, on a large scale, for places
where there was little likelihood of their being
well seen, or for patrons from whom there was
little prospect of rich remuneration. In general,
the best things are done in this way, or else in
the enthusiasm and pride of accomplishing some
great purpose, such as painting a cathedral or a
campo-santo from one end to the other, especially
when the time has been short, and circumstances
disadvantageous.

§ CXXXVII. Works thus executed are of course
despised, on account of their quantity, as well as
their frequent slightness, in the places where they

exist; and they are too large to be portable, and
too vast and comprehensive to be read on the
spot, in the hasty temper of the present age.
They are, therefore, almost universally neglected,
whitewashed by custodes, shot at by soldiers,
suffered to drop from the walls piecemeal in
powder and rags by society in general; but, which
is an advantage more than counterbalancing all
this evil, they are not often "restored." What
is left of them, however fragmentary, however ruinous, however obscured and defiled, is
almost always *the real thing;* there are no fresh
readings: and therefore the greatest treasures of
art which Europe at this moment possesses are
pieces of old plaster on ruinous brick walls, where
the lizards burrow and bask, and which few other
living creatures ever approach; and torn sheets
of dim canvas, in waste corners of churches; and,
mildewed stains, in the shape of human figures,
on the walls of dark chambers, which now and
then an exploring traveller causes to be unlocked
by their tottering custode, looks hastily round,
and retreats from in a weary satisfaction at his
accomplished duty.

§ CXXXVIII. Many of the pictures on the ceilings and walls of the Ducal Palace, by Paul
Veronese and Tintoret, have been more or less
reduced, by neglect, to this condition. Unfortu-
nately, they are not altogether without reputation, and their state has drawn the attention of

the Venetian authorities and academicians. It constantly happens, that public bodies who will not pay five pounds to preserve a picture, will pay fifty to repaint it : * and when I was at Venice in 1846, there were two remedial operations carrying on, at one and the same time, in the two buildings which contain the pictures of greatest value in the city (as pieces of colour, of greatest value in the world), curiously illustrative of this peculiarity in human nature. Buckets were set on the floor of the Scuola di San Rocco in every shower, to catch the rain which came through the pictures of Tintoret on the ceiling; while, in the Ducal Palace, those of Paul Veronese were themselves laid on the floor to be re-painted; and I was myself present at the re-illumination of the breast of a white horse, with a brush, at the end of a stick five feet long, luxuriously dipped in a common house-painter's vessel of paint.

This was, of course, a large picture. The process has already been continued in an

---

* This is easily explained. There are of course, in every place and at all periods, bad painters who conscientiously believe that they can improve every picture they touch ; and these men are generally, in their presumption, the most influential over the innocence, whether of monarchs or municipalities. The carpenter and slater have little influence in recommending the repairs of the roof ; but the bad painter has great influence, as well as interest, in recommending those of the picture,

equally destructive, though somewhat more
delicate manner, over the whole of the humbler
canvases on the ceiling of the Sala del Gran
Consiglio; and I heard it threatened when I
was last in Venice (1851-2) to the "Paradise"
at its extremity, which is yet in tolerable condition,—the largest work of Tintoret, and the
most wonderful piece of pure, manly, and masterly oil-painting in the world.

§ cxxxix. I leave these facts to the consideration of the European patrons of art. Twenty
years hence they will be acknowledged and
regretted; at present I am well aware that it is
of little use to bring them forward, except only
to explain the present impossibility of stating
what pictures *are* and what *were* in the interior
of the Ducal Palace. I can only say that, in
the winter of 1851, the "Paradise" of Tintoret
was still comparatively uninjured, and that the
Camera di Collegio, and its antechamber, and
the Sala de' Pregadi were full of pictures by
Veronese and Tintoret, that made their walls
as precious as so many kingdoms; so precious,
indeed, and so full of majesty, that sometimes
when walking at evening on the Lido, whence
the great chain of the Alps, crested with silver
clouds, might be seen rising above the front of
the Ducal Palace, I used to feel as much awe
in gazing on the building as on the hills, and
could believe that God had done a greater work

in breathing into the narrowness of dust the mighty spirits by whom its haughty walls had been raised, and its burning legends written, than in lifting the rocks of granite higher than the clouds of heaven, and veiling them with their various mantle of purple flower and shadowy pine.

END OF VOL. I.

NOTE.

I HAVE printed the chapter on the Ducal Palace, quite one of the most important pieces of work done in my life, without alteration of its references to the plates of the first edition, because I hope both to republish some of those plates, and, together with them, a few permanent photographs (both from the sculpture of the Palace itself and from my own drawings of its details), which may be purchased by the possessors of this smaller edition to bind with the book or not, as they please. This separate publication I can now soon get set in hand ; and I believe it will cause much less confusion to leave for the present the references to the old plates untouched. The wood-blocks used for the first three figures in this chapter are the original ones : that of the Ducal Palace façade was drawn on the wood by my own hand, and cost me more trouble than it is worth, being merely given for division and proportion. The greater part of the first volume omitted in this edition after " The Quarry," will be re-published in the series of my reprinted works, with its original wood-blocks.*

* Since this note was written, the work has been reprinted in complete form, with all the illustrations, as formerly issued. (*Publisher's note*, 1888.)

But my mind is mainly set now on getting some worthy illustration of the St. Mark's mosaics, and of such remains of the old capitals (now for ever removed, in process of the Palace restoration, from their life in sea wind and sunlight, and their ancient duty, to a museum-grave) as I have useful record of, drawn in their native light. The series, both of these and of the earlier mosaics, of which the sequence is sketched in the preceding volume, and farther explained in the third number of "St. Mark's Rest," become to me every hour of my life more precious both for their art and their meaning ; and if any of my readers care to help me, in my old age, to fulfil my life's work rightly, let them send what pence they can spare for these objects to my publisher, Mr. Allen, Sunnyside, Orpington, Kent.

Since writing the first part of this note, I have received a letter from Mr. Burne Jones, assuring me of his earnest sympathy in its object, and giving me hope even of his superintendence of the drawings, which I have already desired to be undertaken. But I am no longer able to continue work of this kind at my own cost ; and the fulfilment of my purpose must entirely depend on the money-help given me by my readers.

Printed by BALLANTYNE, HANSON & CO
London and Edinburgh